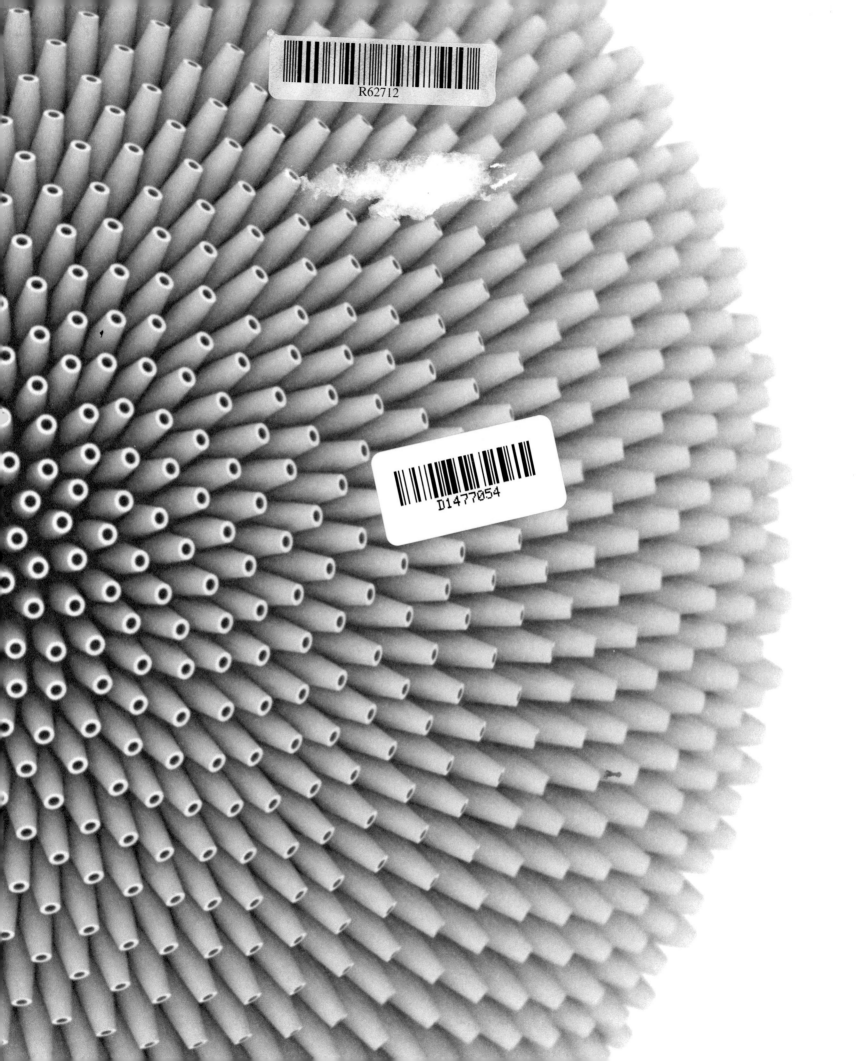

Made Of...

New Materials Sourcebook for Architecture and Design

Christiane Sauer

gestalten

Content

Introduction

— Christiane Sauer

Architecture is more than an organized agglomeration of construction materials. It communicates a sense of space and of the activities that are to take place in it. This idea is expressed not only in the form and structure of the building but also in the surfaces that act as a visible layer and enclose the space or create the outer frontage.

Planning means combining various materials in a meaningful manner to ensure that a building capable of functioning according to design, economic, and technical parameters results. In terms of actual practice, the architect is faced with a constantly increasing choice of materials on the global market. Innovations such as nanotechnology or computer-controlled production techniques are now reaching the construction industry. Developments from aircraft and motor-vehicle manufacturing are being adapted to an increasing extent by designers and architects as a means of producing complex forms efficiently. To keep abreast of developments and be aware of the sheer variety of materials and methods that are available is already a full-time task that tends to overstretch the day-to-day working capacity of an architect's office or design studio.

This book is intended as a guide to new technologies and as a source of both information and inspiration. It penetrates deeper than the superficial as the word is commonly understood, and emphasizes the architectural design opportunities offered by innovations in materials. The material itself may be the starting point for a draft concept, or the latter may demand a material that interprets it adequately. Materials dealt with here could supply inspiration for new applications, but examples of innovative architectural and design projects that already use these materials or technologies are also described. The selected examples reveal the full bandwidth of new developments in materials and technologies as well as their architectural relevance for design and construction. The chapters are geared to architectural topics that are closely related to actual practice, for example spatial continuity, energy-generating surfaces, and materials suitable for recycling. Central questions relating to form generation and efficient use of materials are a recurrent topic throughout the book.

Efficiency of materials

A material can be regarded as efficient if it is available in the form that best suits its intended purpose. Structural efficiency, for example, means achieving maximum strength or rigidity with minimum use of materials. Functional efficiency is to be found in the technical layers of the building's envelope, which fulfil their protective function against climatic influences and wear despite steadily reduced material thicknesses or by means of technical

coatings in the micro or nano size range. Inside buildings, external lighting or climate control elements have been rendered obsolete by new surfaces that perform the relevant technical tasks and, as spatial-functional material hybrids, are progressing toward the status of an intelligent environment.

An example of efficiency in the sense of sustainable and economical use of resources is provided by energy-generating surfaces that convert sunlight into electricity; in optimal conditions they not only supply the building to which they are attached but also produce excess electrical current. In this way, future buildings may even become energy suppliers rather than energy consumers. Efficiency in the recovery of raw materials can be improved by recycling materials or returning them to the utilization process. The construction industry is still one of the largest producers of waste. Although building-industry products have relatively lengthy life-cycles, large quantities have to be disposed of in due course. The nature of building scrap depends on the construction method that was used. We could be said to be planning tomorrow's ruins today. The initial choice of material and construction method determines whether the end result is hazardous waste or a source of new raw material. Renewable materials for insulation or those derived from vegetable fibers and used for structural purposes also have considerable potential for building work; they can be produced with very low primary energy consumption, possess good technical properties, and cause no disposal problems.

Innovations in materials

The product-neutral material descriptions in the chapters that follow are focused on the presentation of new technologies that can be adapted to suit individual design demands. Many manufacturers have supplied useful information and pictures on this topic, and are listed as references in the appendix. The range of examples extends from innovative "smart materials"—that is to say those which can react to stimuli in their environment, with a structure enabling them to adapt to various utilization scenarios—to traditional techniques that have now been revived, such as the carbonization of wood surfaces to render them more durable. Some of the innovations concerning materials are still at the development stage and have not yet reached the market. In such cases prototypes or experiments with materials are described and accompanied by technical background information, with the aim of stimulating further thinking and encouraging the exploration of new potential uses in a construction-industry context.

A new "design vocabulary" will only arise from knowledge of the fundamental technologies that are involved. These will not necessarily come from hi-tech fields: innovations are often based on the intelligent utilization of structures or physical properties already inherent in the material—which implies working with, rather than in opposition to the material. It is remarkable how many new aspects of seemingly well-known materials are constantly being discovered.

If articles fabricated from sheet metal, for example, are exposed to air or water pressure, the surface curvature will automatically correspond to the material's technical parameters. This has a stabilizing effect similar to folding or beading, but with the advantage that the process can be carried out without complex forming tools, and the new stabilizing shape has its own visual appeal derived from the material.

Investigation of the cell structure of such a traditional material as wood, which man has worked for several thousand years, has also led to new approaches. Special bending techniques made possible by manipulation of the wood fibers now permit timber scantlings to be processed into hollow profiles with efficient stress analysis values but with dimensions no longer tied to the geometry of the mature timber. In this way even poor-quality wood residues can undergo efficient further processing, with the result that scarcely any waste remains after the timber has been processed.

Even if a specific property of a material has hitherto been regarded as negative, a new application may be found that makes positive use of it. If wood is allowed to swell, an adaptive surface can be created, with wooden veneer elements that curve when exposed to increasing atmospheric humidity. If this property were to be used in the wet rooms of buildings, the openings caused by the action of the material could perform a ventilating function without needing an external energy source. This approach makes use of the material's own logic, that is to say the material itself possesses all the necessary functional characteristics.

Technology transfer

Adapting biological principles for technical applications is an increasingly frequent source of inspiration for designers. Many of the new materials have parallels in nature. Extremely rigid, lightweight metallic foam structures have been inspired by bones; the honeycomb panel principle, which can be extended almost at will as a structural element, has been borrowed from the beehive. New fastening techniques are based on the surface of burrs or of gecko's feet. Bionics has emerged as a transfer science from the cross-pollination of biology and engineering. Each of these branches of science profits from the other and has been able to make new discoveries.

Nature is of course not the only source of inspiration for architectural innovation. Dialog with engineers from the aviation, space-travel, or motor-vehicle industries has led to innovative concepts that benefit from the weight-saving designs and efficient use of materials customary in vehicle and aircraft construction. There are already several interesting cooperation projects in which designers utilize high-tech industrial manufacturing technologies in order to develop new approaches to design and construction. As in other fields, it is becoming more and more important for the manufacturing and transportation of construction materials to consume as little energy as possible. The lower the weight of a structure, the smaller the dimensions of the foundations and the connecting elements.

Material transfer offering new design prospects in the low-tech area is in the tradition of "objets trouvés," with materials being transferred to a new, unfamiliar context. Although the material remains the same, the "instructions for use" are changed. Metal conveyor belts become sunblinds, for instance, or roof seals are transformed into a waterproof skin for a building. In the re-use design process, the form and function of materials can also inspire architects to develop new applications for them.

Planning processes

To some extent the adoption of new materials and technologies is always an experiment, and can only be implemented in a very specific environment. The first requirement is vision on the part of the planner, that is to say the will to investigate new design and structural potential that goes beyond anything available in the product catalogs. Next, the client must be prepared to pursue paths in the construction area that have still not been fully explored. Long-term test results are still not available for many materials. In the plastics and coatings areas, in which new compounds are constantly being created, the verifiable empirical results, for instance those concerning resistance to weather effects, usually go back no more than a few years. In many cases, technical approval for new applications of materials must be obtained by individual testing.

In contrast to this, highly individual draft designs have become much easier to implement now that computer-aided planning and manufacturing processes can be used. Even geometrically complex construction elements can today be produced relatively easily. Direct digital communication between the planning data file and production machinery makes it possible to increase the efficiency of production sequences and avoid possible sources of error. In this area the tendency is away from the classic construction site, the success of which depends on the craft skills of the personnel working on it, and toward a complete, pre-determined planning process which merely calls for prefabricated structural elements to be assembled on site. While this cuts construction time, the planning phases become correspondingly more intensive and include the complex information management needed to maintain the vast quantities of data that define the complex geometries of the individually formed parts.

Material and surface

The current revival of ornamental forms and patterned surfaces can be justified in view of the new technical opportunities described above. It has become easy to compose individual motifs and cut, mill, or print the surfaces by means of CNC technology. This enables surfaces to demonstrate a new graphic element. Façades of this kind convert the carcass of the building into an information display and marketing tool, but can easily be replaced when required if the structure is made up of the necessary layers. Fashion-driven changes and corporate identity are beginning to play a more and more central role. "Media façades" are becoming more and more popular, and provide two effects at the same time: the building's appearance can be changed at will, and the frontages can be programmed to display different contents.

Will surfaces therefore become more "superficial"? This is certainly true from a technical standpoint, if we consider the micro- and nano-coatings that can no longer even be seen with the naked eye. The material's authenticity is no longer a factor: steel can be protected against scratching by a nano-glass surface, but we still have the feeling that we are touching metal. Exposed concrete can create an impression of solidity, but be rendered translucent in a few moments by integrated light-conducting fibers. "Intelligent" systems, as they are known, can also be incorporated invisibly into the surfaces: they assess and respond to information on room condition or usage. Walls begin to glow as night falls, windows darken when hit by sunlight and flooring materials transmit alarm signals in an emergency. The aim of this "ambient intelligence" is for it to be unnoticed when integrated into spatial elements and to permit intuitive use: the room must seem to respond by itself to our needs.

Designed surfaces, however, are always in a contextual and conceptual relationship with the spaces they create. They can reinforce a design concept or act in opposition to it, but the relationship is always there. In its absence they would be no more than an interchangeable gimmick and would lose their spatial or functional relevance.

Although the over-informed world in which we live subjects us to a continuous flood of day-to-day impressions, there have been recent signs of an increased demand for surfaces that can be experienced sensually. We can for instance identify a current fascination with haptic three-dimensional surfaces or with mysteriously shimmering translucent materials. These surfaces can tell us a story, and no matter how many grandiose technical innovations become available, will never lose their fascination and their significance. They too are dealt with in this book. Let yourself be inspired!

A
8 – 41

Light and Strong

1 — Buckminster Fuller, Dymaxion Car and Fly's Eye Dome made of glass-fiber-reinforced plastic.

0.0 Technology Transfer

Efficiency, sustainability, and economy are what we expect of the new generation of materials. Today, the leading pioneers in the development of innovative materials are the creative design labs of the highly competitive automotive and aerospace industries. In the design of mobile structures, paramount importance is attached to low weight and structural strength. But the same ultra-light and high-tensile materials deployed in these industries can also provide new approaches to sophisticated architectural concepts.

However, it can often take years or even decades for a material that was developed in the high-tech industry to be transformed into a marketable construction product. Either there is a failure to recognize the immediate potential of technology transfer, or there is a reluctance to invest in the time-consuming and expensive procedures necessary to obtain permission for architectural purposes.

Yet when it comes to the environmental impact of a building, weight plays an increasingly significant role. Lightweight constructions require less material, save fuel on transport to the building site, and can be designed with smaller assembly fittings. Even the foundations can be minimized to consume less resources. Materials that are light, flexible, and strong are also needed for temporary constructions such as mobile accommodation and trade-fair structures.

These requirements are fulfilled by composite materials such as sandwich panels or fiber-reinforced materials that can be precisely dimensioned to their specific task, thereby saving material.

Already in 1930, the architect and engineer Buckminster Fuller was raising the question as to how much a building should actually weigh. Drawing his inspiration partly from nature and partly from the latest technologies in shipbuilding and aircraft construction, he demanded that minimum levels of energy and material consumption be used to achieve maximum levels of structural efficiency. This led not only to the design of lightweight, transportable building structures, but also to vehicles such as the Dymaxion Car—an automobile designed according to aerodynamic principles that he developed in collaboration with a yacht builder. At the same time, Fuller was always looking for new materials that could satisfy his demand for stability, flexibility, and low weight. He made use of the lightweight and extremely strong metal alloy duralumin, for example, and in later building projects he used fiber-reinforced plastics.[1]

In the mid-1960s, there was a renewed boom in plastic buildings. Revolutionary design ideas were in the air and technological mile-

2 — The Futuro House developed by Finnish architect Matti Suuronen in 1968 was initially designed as a transportable ski cabin. Its external shape resembles a UFO, while the name underlines its futuristic style. The Futuro can be transported to its location by helicopter. Developed for mass production, the 50 m² building consists of sandwich elements with an insulating polyurethane core and facing of glass-fiber-reinforced plastic. Futuro House, Finland, 1968. Architecture: Matti Suuronen.

3 — DAX Dining Armchair, 1948. Design: Charles & Ray Eames, California.

stones such as the moon landing had fired up the creative imagination of architects and designers. Affordable and transportable prefabricated houses were developed that could supposedly be deployed irrespective of context to provide space for new living concepts. Plastic elements that were lightweight and cheap to mass produce were the order of the day. Dozens of houses—most of them single-storey—were designed from plastic, although none of them ever broke through to a broader market. Perhaps unresolved structural issues played a role here, along with a lack of acceptance for the aesthetic language and the rising prices caused by the oil crisis of the 1970s, which made the material unattractive for the construction industry.[2]

In product and furniture design—unlike in architecture—the transfer of the latest material developments to new contexts can be done quickly and without long approval procedures. This is not even a particularly recent phenomenon.

Towards the end of the 1940s, Charles and Ray Eames abandoned their original plan of using sheet metal for the DAX Dining Armchair and opted instead for a material that was still new to design at that point—**glass-fiber-reinforced polymer** (GRP). This composite material was something they had discovered in the military. During the Second World War, GRP was used to make robust, radar-permeable coverings for aircraft noses. But not only did the Eameses utilize the structural characteristics of the material, they also created an entirely new aesthetic by leaving the plastic of the chair shell in a raw state with its glass fiber openly visible. The focus here is on the free-form shape and smooth surface of the material, with the reinforcing fiber evenly spread through the plastic.[3]

4 — Demonstration object of a fuselage shell woven from carbon fiber with a window opening, Institute of Aircraft Design (IFB), University of Stuttgart.

5 — Carbon Chair, 2004. Design: Bertjan Pot and Marcel Wanders, Moooi, Netherlands.

Today, the extremely lightweight and high-tensile material of **carbon fiber** has replaced glass fiber in aircraft construction. Using specific calculations, the fiber orientation is precisely tailored to the specific load capacity, and the thickness of the weave is dimensioned accordingly. Building elements are integrally joined by interweaving or stitching them together prior to lamination, thus eliminating the risk of breaking or loosening that can occur with rivets and screws. Even openings in the material, such as windows in the fuselage, are no longer a potential weakness but are constructed with reinforcements of appropriate strength to the load.[4]

The fiber itself has thus become a structural tool—an aspect that was put to creative use by designers Bertjan Pot and Marcel Wanders in their Carbon Chair. This piece of furniture consists entirely of carbon fiber impregnated with epoxy resin. Although the fiber orientation in the seating surface appears random, the varying density of the mesh actually reflects the load. The chair creates an extremely vivid and lightweight impression.[5] In contrast to the smooth surface of the DAX chair, the fiber here becomes a structural, form-giving, and design element.

The aesthetic and functional potential contained in the transfer of technology to new contexts is huge, although dialog between the various disciplines is essential. Numerous successful examples already exist, including, but not limited to, fiber-reinforced polymers.

One example is the whole new scientific field of biomimetics, which has arisen from the dialog between biology and technology—ranging from high-speed swimsuits with surfaces that imitate the texture of shark skin, to stable honeycombs transposed into new contexts on various scales as construction systems.

1.0 Reinforced

Structural efficiency is one of the core demands placed on contemporary materials. A material is efficient if its internal structure is optimally adapted to its purpose, thereby allowing the amount of material to be minimized. In the production and deployment of materials on construction sites, resources should be consumed as sparingly as possible. Composite materials fulfill this demand because they are made up of materials with differing characteristics, with the combined materials performing better than as individual components. Examples of structurally efficient materials include steel-reinforced and fiber-reinforced materials, as well as sandwich systems.

Material composites are not a new idea. "Opus caementicium"—the cementitious building material used by the Romans —was mixed with plant fiber or animal hair to improve its mechanical properties. In the 19th century, the French gardener Joseph Monier decided to strengthen his cement flowerpots by fitting

6 — ECC (Engineered Cementitious Composite) concrete is capable of ductile deformation thanks to its synthetic fiber reinforcement and can even self-repair hairline fractures. Development: University of Michigan, Prof. Victor Li, Ann Arbor, USA.

them with wire mesh. The principle proved to be extremely successful. He registered the idea as a patent, thus inventing the forerunner to one of the modern world's most ubiquitous materials—reinforced concrete.

Today, engineers working with **concrete** can enhance its mechanical properties and minimize cracks by using textiles or fibers made of steel, plastic, or glass to transmit the tensile forces. In certain cases, the fibers can even replace steel reinforcement entirely. The new reinforcements also enable significant improvements in the "ductility" of concrete.

At the University of Michigan, microscopic plastic fibers have been developed that make concrete as bendable as metal. The material is 40% lighter and 500 times more crack-resistant than conventional concrete. Steel reinforcements in the material can be massively reduced or even eliminated. The revolutionary material ECC (Engineered Cementitious Composite) is based on the fact that the **cement** in the material "glides" along specially coated fibers, thus avoiding breakages when the composite is deformed. This material can significantly reduce maintenance and inspection costs in the long term—particularly on bridge structures and earthquake-proof buildings—because no cracks will form that demand renovation. Hairline fractures are healed by the material

Reinforced

itself: The dry and fractured material exposed by the crack reacts with rainwater and carbon dioxide to form "scar tissue." Calcium carbonate is produced here, automatically and permanently sealing the fissure.[6]

Fiber-reinforced polymers

Polymers are highly suitable for serving as a basis for fiber-reinforced material composites. The fibers are embedded in a (usually polyester, epoxy, or vinylester-based) resin matrix that transmits the compressive and shear forces. Load calculations enable the fiber orientation to be precisely adapted to operational need. The fibers can be woven, looped, wound, or braided, depending on the structural requirements and the desired form. Because the fibers are permanently embedded within the polymer matrix during production, the raw materials cannot be separated back out for recycling purposes. The widely used **thermosetting resins** can only be disposed of via shredding and usage as fuel (incineration).

Fiber-reinforced polymers inhabit an immense field that extends from plant-based biocomposites, via translucent materials with embedded glass fiber, right through to high-performance and ultra-high-tensile carbon-fiber-reinforced polymers. Polymer composites are already omnipresent in the automobile and aerospace industries, in shipbuilding, and in wind turbine construction. Apart from their structural properties, the materials also have considerable design potential for architectural applications.

But in the construction industry there are currently no binding technical guidelines for the dimensioning of load-bearing fibrous polymer building elements. This means that approval for the structural and fire behavior of such elements must be obtained on a case-by-case basis. In order to evaluate fire behavior, the entire material complex must always be taken into account, with due consideration given to the specific polymer formula and the fiber material. The fire resistance of a material can be improved by the application of flame retardants.
— **"Fiber-reinforced polymers (FRPs)" page 40**

1.1 Glass fiber

Glass-fiber-reinforced polymers (GRP) are extremely resilient. The materials have insulating properties, can be equipped with UV and fire resistance, and do not decompose. They are prefabricated in the form of sheets or profiles.

GRP sheet material provides a low-cost façade covering that opens up a broad range of design options. The material can be fabricated in large formats, enabling the installation process to be completed much more quickly. Sheets measuring 2.5 x 4 m or planks measuring 0.5 cm x 15 m can be manufactured without difficulty.

Using **pultrusion processes**, it is also possible to fabricate different profiles. The finished products can serve as load-bearing floor elements or structural façade elements, for example.[11, 13]

Individual designs can be generated either in unique one-off pieces or longer production runs. Here, negative molds are fabricated in which glass fiber reinforcement and resin are laminated together according to structural requirements. GRP is interesting from a design perspective because it can assume any color and can be produced in the entire spectrum from opaque to translucent.[7-9, 12]

7 — Glass-fiber mats in production.

8 — GRP laminating process.

9 — Polypropylene sandwich panel with translucent facing that is glass-fiber-reinforced.

With the correct dimensioning, load-bearing GRP profiles need only a fraction of the material that equivalent steel constructions require. The first profile geometries to be developed closely resembled their steel counterparts and used similar sections. But because a kilogram of the composite is about ten times more expensive than a kilogram of steel, material-appropriate design with minimized use of materials is highly advantageous. The load-bearing performance depends on the orientation of the embedded fibers— like with reinforced concrete. As a structural material, GRP is now even used in bridge building.[15]

10 — Large GRP façade panels at the Fiberline factory and company headquarters in Middelfart, Denmark. Architecture: Jan Søndergaard of KHR Architekter, Copenhagen.

11 — Pultrusion facility for manufacturing GRP profiles. The reinforcement material is continuously drawn through the forming equipment and then impregnated with resin.

At the Institute of Building Structures and Structural Design (ITKE) at the University of Stuttgart, flat load-bearing profiles made of GRP have been developed as an alternative to conventional aluminum profiles. These are bonded to stepped insulating glazing units, whereby the bond also serves the structural purposes of transmitting wind loads and securing the panels against deflection. The construction is simple and minimizes the dimensions of the framing, making it possible to achieve lines that are extremely slender and elegant.[14]

Several window manufacturers already offer energy-saving window profiles made of GRP or GRP/wood combinations. Thanks to the minimal use of materials, excellent insulating properties, and long lifespan, glass-fiber-reinforced polymers even facilitate the construction of energy-efficient buildings that conform to the "passive house" standard.

— **"Manufacturing processes for fiber-reinforced plastic (FRP) elements" page 40**

13 — 12 km of elliptical GRP profiles were interwoven in a traditional willow fence pattern to form a façade screen for the Palacio de Congresos in the Spanish city of Badajoz. The circular wall measures 75 meters in diameter and is 14 meters high. The façade is designed to easily withstand temperature fluctuations and wind loads. Badajoz Convention Center, Spain, 2006. Architecture: José Selgas and Lucía Cano, Madrid. Consulting engineers: Pedelta Structural Engineers, Barcelona. Development: Fiberline Composites, Denmark.

12 — For a 350 meter long pavilion entitled Forum Soft at Expo 2002 in Switzerland, a material was sought that needed to be colored, translucent, inexpensive, and light enough to allow the efficient fabrication of an internal and external roofing layer covering 48,000 m². The solution was U-shaped profiles, 80 cm wide and up to 12 m long, made of red translucent GRP. These were fitted to the roof surface in a shingle-type arrangement. The roof construction of lenticular beams was lined on the underside with the same material, creating a roof surface that is homogenous and luminous in appearance. The plastic skin is extremely thin and lightweight due to the choice of material. At just 2 mm thick, it weighs only 3 kg/m². Forum Soft, Arteplage Yverdon, Switzerland, 2002. Architecture: Vehovar & Jauslin, Zurich, Mühlemann & Partner, Grenchen.

14 — Glass/GRP composite construction for façade profiles. Development: Institute of Building Structures and Structural Design (ITKE) at the University of Stuttgart, Prof. Jan Knippers, Dr. Ing. Stefan Peters.

15 — Large picture: Bridge to the Blur Building, Yverdon-les-Bains, Switzerland, 2002. Architecture: Diller Scofidio + Renfro, NYC/Dirk Hebel, Zurich.

Small picture: 90% of the pedestrian bridge near Winterthur in Switzerland is made of GRP. Only the screws and the tension rods used in the construction process are made of steel. A thin-walled ovoid plastic beam with considerable height provides the structural support. Brace elements at the ends of the individual segments are bolted together. Spanning 16 meters, the bridge weighs just 850 kg and can be set up in under two hours. Rather than using con-

crete foundations, it is stabilized by simply digging the structure into the ground on site. Originally devised by the Swiss Army as an emergency bridge, the construction was later revised for a high-profile purpose—serving as the bridge to Diller & Scofidio's cloud installation at the Swiss Expo 2002. The 250 meter long plastic walkway easily withstood the constant load of hundreds of thousands of visitors.
Lightweight emergency bridge made of GRP. Design & development: Staubli, Kurath und Partner, Zurich/Swissfiber AG, Zurich.

16 — The GRP façade panels of the Danish church "Hellig Kors" are just 4 mm thick and fitted with bars on the back that clip onto a substructure. The surface is finished with a UV-resistant synthetic resin that protects the panels against weathering.
Apart from the surface, GRP was also used to produce load-bearing profiles and frames for double glazing. Here, use is made of the fact that GRP has a similar thermal expansion coefficient to glass on account of its high glass-fiber content, allowing the bonded materials to act together without stress. Furthermore, the insulating GRP ensures

that no thermal bridges can occur at the window profiles. This is a decisive advantage over conventional metal constructions.
Hellig Kors Kirke, Jyllinge, 2008. Architecture: KHR Architekter, Copenhagen.
— see pages 16/17

Reinforced – Glass fiber

17 — Evidence that contemporary plastics are no longer solely associated with purely industrial surfaces is provided by a church in the Danish town of Jyllinge. The sculptural construction is covered in a homogenous skin of 50 cm-wide GRP panels that line the surface with a fine velvety sheen. Backed with a translucent layer of thermal insulation made of cellulose, the translucent GRP roofing layer subtly filters the light as it enters the church interior. The permanently changing interplay of light and shadow is intensified by the different angles of the building's surface.

Hellig Kors Kirke, Jyllinge, 2008. Architecture: KHR Architekter, Copenhagen.

— see page 15

Reinforced – Glass fiber

1.2 Carbon fiber

If high load capacities are required, carbon fibers are the right choice—they have around 15 times the tensile strength of steel. Furthermore, the weight of **carbon-fiber-reinforced polymer** (CRP) is around 30% less than aluminum. Thus, materials can be created that are extremely lightweight and yet resilient, making carbon fiber composites a particularly interesting option for motor racing and aircraft construction, where every saved kilogram helps to increase efficiency and reduce fuel costs. Carbon already accounts for one quarter of the material on modern aircraft such as the Airbus A380.

During production, the fiber orientation can be precisely tailored to match the expected forces. To get the fibers into the desired shape, the textile reinforcements are fabricated using techniques such as structural weaving, braiding, sewing, and stitching before being impregnated with resin and fixed. The sewing or weaving can also be done three-dimensionally with the help of special computer-guided machines and robots. A further property of carbon is its electrical conductivity, which can be used to operate sensors, integrated LEDs and other functional components.

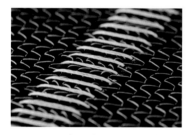

18 — Carbon-fiber fabric in aircraft construction. Several layers of carbon-fiber fabric are stitched together with aramid fiber in a tufting process before being impregnated with resin and cured to form a high-strength composite. Development: Institute of Aircraft Design (IFB), University of Stuttgart.

The technique of overbraiding allows three-dimensional CRP elements to be produced in series. Robots push a raw model core of the desired geometry through a circular machine that is several meters in diameter and resembles a gigantic spider's web. This web is loaded with threads of carbon, polyester, or glass fiber that are woven around the raw shape in a computer-controlled process. The braiding is then impregnated with resin and thermally cured.[19]

One step further up the dimensional scale, the architects Peter Testa and Devyn Weiser translated the idea of woven structures onto a high-rise office building that is designed to take full advantage of the high-tensile strength of carbon fiber and requires no conventional building materials such as steel, glass, and concrete. Although it has not yet been realized, the design has already been calculated by Arup engineers and it represents an interesting contribution to visionary construction technology.

The net-like exterior structure of the 40-storey building consists of a pre-compressed double helix structure of interlacing

19 — The Dutch designer Wieki Somers experimented with an overbraiding technique borrowed from aircraft construction in order to produce a lamp made of glass fiber and carbon fiber that was woven by 144 computer-guided spindles. The object contains no electric cables and the LEDs woven into the lampshade are illuminated via the electricity-conducting properties of the carbon fiber. Bellflower, 2007. Design: Wieki Somers in collaboration with TU Delft.

fiber strands. The floors measure 38 meters in diameter and are "woven" into the vertical elements so that the load-bearing structure is homogenous rather than hierarchical, with all the structural parts acting together.

The maintenance of this kind of building could be simplified by a network of sensors woven into the matrix, monitoring the integrity of all the structural members throughout their lifespan and detecting any problems in real time.

Fuel costs for transportation are minimized by the reduction in weight and volume of the building materials. Only fiber and resin need to be delivered to the construction site—the building is woven on site using mobile pultrusion machines. The completion time is also much shorter than for conventional projects.[21]

Carbon fiber can also be laminated onto structurally weaker materials to reinforce them. At the Institute of Aircraft Design in Stuttgart, tests were conducted to improve the structural strength of conventional **fiberboards** (1 m long and 5 cm wide) against breakage using just 10 grams of carbon fiber. This approach has interesting technical and design implications, particularly for the field of building renovation.[22]

20 — The featherweight construction of this seating object is woven from carbon fiber. The flexible mesh behaves in a cushioning manner.
Spun Chaise, 2003. Design: Mathias Bengtsson, London/Stockholm.

21 — The vision of a high-rise tower woven from carbon: The vertical CRP profiles with rectangular sections of 3 x 30 cm are produced on site by robotic pultrusion machines that continuously work their way up and along the carbon bundles, pressing them into shape and impregnating them with resin. By interweaving all the structural elements, continuous strands of carbon fiber are produced that extend over the entire height of the tower. Filament, wound ramps that weave in and out of the primary structure provide lateral bracing. Serving as both building envelope and thermal barrier is a double-layered transparent plastic membrane. Due to this thermal barrier, energy consumption has been calculated as being 50% less than in high-rise structures with conventional air conditioning.
Carbon Tower, 2001–2004. Architecture: TESTA, Peter Testa, Devyn Weiser, Los Angeles. Consulting Engineers: Arup, New York.

22 — Carbon fiber stitched onto pressboard strips to strengthen the structural characteristics. Development: Institute of Aircraft Design (IFB), University of Stuttgart, Dipl. Des. Gerd Falk.

Reinforced – Carbon fiber

23 — A chair light enough to be picked up by a child with one finger was Shigeru Ban's intention when creating this minimalistic chair. Carbon fiber provides great tensile strength but loses out on compressive strength. The design makes use of the material's advantages and avoids its disadvantages by sticking a 0.25 mm layer of carbon fabric onto both sides of a 1.5 mm aluminum panel. The resulting composite has a thickness of only 2 mm and is highly stable under loads and easy to work with. The rims are set on edge to lend the legs greater stability. The chair was designed for the Tokyo Fiber "Senseware" exhibition, 2009.
Carbon Fiber Chair, Tokyo, 2009. Design: Shigeru Ban in cooperation with Cassina.

Reinforced – Carbon fiber

1.3 Natural fiber

The relatively new **biocomposites** combine extremely light and stable plant fiber with a matrix of conventional or biodegradable polymers. Based on raw materials that are renewable, this group of materials is continuing to gain significance.

If the structure of wood is examined in detail, it too reveals itself to be a biocomposite system. Wood mainly consists of lignin—a natural polymer that is the filling and support material that gives trees their compressive strength. Embedded within this

matrix are countless directionally aligned fibers made of **cellulose** that transmit tensile forces. Acting together, this natural high-performance composite material supports the load of soaring branches and can withstand the huge tensile forces of storms.

24 — "Schaukel-Fauteuil No. 1" by Thonet, 1860, Design: Michael Thonet and son

The Thonet Brothers made use of the internal structure of this "natural composite" 150 years ago with their bent wood furniture. In the bending process, the lignin is softened with heat and water before being deformed in the fiber direction and fixed into its new position. The fibers thus follow and stabilize the desired shape, enabling the cross sections of the material to be minimized.[24]

25 — Biocomposite of woven linen and hemp with polyester resin.

The tensile strength in natural-fiber-reinforced polymers is provided by plants such as **cotton**, **flax**, **hemp**, and **jute**. The surrounding matrix can either be made from conventional **synthetic thermosetting and thermoplastic materials** or produced on a natural basis with vegetable starch, lignin, or vegetable oils. This means that high-performance polymers can now be produced without the inevitable use of mineral oil. In future, they will be grown in fields. From a design perspective, the surfaces of biocomposites have a definite appeal, in that the reinforcing plant fibers remain clearly visible, making a clear statement about the material's origin.[25, 26]

While natural-fiber-reinforced polymers have until now been mostly used as concealed substrate materials, they are gradually liberating themselves for design applications. The pattern-

26 — The material Nabasco combines natural fibers such as hemp and flax with conventional resins such as polyester and epoxy. In future, it should also be available with bio resins. The material can be used for a wide range of aesthetic purposes—including for exposed surfaces.

27 — Sanitary units made of the biocomposite Nabasco. The surface of hemp, flax, and sisal mixed with a semi-transparent polyester resin and white pigment shows off the natural fiber content of the material. Design: Faro Architects, Netherlands.

ing and feel of the material can be showcased as coming from a natural product while meeting the expectations of contemporary design.[27]

Because of their low density and high-tensile strength, natural fibers can significantly reduce the weight of a building element in comparison with glass fiber. Natural-fiber-reinforced polymers are up to 30 % lighter than conventional fiber composites, translating into significant reductions in fuel consumption and therefore CO_2 emissions if used in vehicle or aircraft construction. Furthermore, the energy consumption required to manufacture renewable plant fiber is several times less than glass or carbon fiber.

Even the prototypes of a regatta catamaran and a racing car have been built using flax-fiber composites. Apart from being water and weatherproof, the materials used here also needed to meet the highest safety requirements.[28]

Another sustainable fiber option is the natural product of **basalt fiber**. It lies between glass and carbon fiber in terms of quality, and is resistant to heat and chemicals. It is also significantly cheaper than carbon, making it suitable for the mass market.[29]

To make optimum use of the characteristics that fiber composite materials offer, form and function need to be designed in an integrated fashion from the very start of the development process. The point is that fiber composites are not a finished material, but rather a technology that can be adapted to individual requirements.

The variable parameters in terms of form and structure make it essential for planners, engineers, and manufacturers to collaborate from the outset. The resulting building elements are extremely cost-effective, structurally efficient, and allow highly individual expression in their design.

28 — The bodywork components of the BioConcept-Car are made from a flax-cotton textile previously impregnated with linseed oil acrylate. The flax fiber provides the stability, while the cotton is elastic and better at absorbing impacts.

29 — Basalt fiber.

30 — Natural-fiber fleece for deployment in vehicle construction.

Reinforced – Natural fiber

31 — As part of the Green Architecture for the Future exhibition at the Louisiana Museum of Modern Art, the Danish architects 3XN built a pavilion using biocomposites. Flax fiber was mixed with biological resin based on corn starch and soya oil. The inner core of the sandwich construction was made from cork sheets.
Louisiana Pavilion, Denmark, 2009.
Architecture: 3XN, A/S, Copenhagen.

2.0 Sandwiches

Sandwich materials are both lightweight and stable with good insulating properties. These **composites** can fulfill a range of structural and functional building requirements such as thermal and acoustic insulation or translucency. With sandwich materials, the facing is joined together with the inner core material to create a stable composite. Facings made of aluminum, paper, fiber-reinforced plastic, or even wood can be combined with cores of optional thickness. The core itself can be made of foam materials or honeycombs of metal, paper, or plastic, depending on the specific requirements. The materials can be customized in their appearance and stability.[32, 35]

Standard **wood** products for building can also be based on the sandwich principle—high-grade veneer and a lightweight core. Classic solid-core panels are an example of this. With the layers acting together, the material becomes rigid but retains its light weight. For panels with particularly large dimensions, one suitable core material is balsa—the lightest of all the timbers. The panels provide both acoustic and thermal insulation, are extremely resistant to pressure due to the vertical fibers in the middle layer, and can be coated with veneers and other common surface materials. Even in the possible dimensions of up to 210 x 520 cm and up to 10 cm thick, the panels remain easy to handle thanks to their low weight.[33]

32 — Sandwich panels.

33 — With their lightweight balsa cores and light poplar plywood facing, these sandwich panels weigh 25 % less than conventional wood panels.

If several material layers are combined, "laminated materials" are the result. One common example is plywood, in which wood layers are glued together with their grains perpendicular to each other to create a stress-free composite where the layers stabilize each other against deformation. Interesting visual effects can be created within the cross section by replacing layers with plant fiber, for example.[34]

Room-high sandwich panels can also be processed into thermally insulating and stable exterior wall elements. In this case, the inner core is made of foamed plastics such as **polyurethane** or **expanded polystyrene** while the facings are made of wood, aluminum, or fiber-reinforced plastic that is laminated on.[36]

— "Sandwiches" page 41

34 — Kirei Board consists of 90 % reclaimed sorghum stalks. Left over from the annual sorghum harvest, the stalk material is layered in a composite.

35 — Insulating panels with layers of GRP laminated on.

36 — Using all-in-one walls, the Spacebox is a transportable accommodation module that updates the plug-in housing concepts of the 1960s. Each of the combinable housing units consists of a window and five prefabricated panels (two for the walls, one each for the ceiling, floor, and rear). The panels have an insulating and fire-resistant core of Resol foam, covered on both sides by layers of 3 mm thick glass-fiber-reinforced <u>polyester</u> facing. This sandwich of materials is infused with resin via a vacuum injection process. The plastic surface can be manufactured in any RAL color. The interior walls are fitted with additional cement-based fire-retardant panels coated with gypsum plaster.
Deployed until now as minimal housing and student accommodation, the room boxes are transported to site by truck and lowered into place by crane. This means that inexpensive living space can be made available at short notice wherever it is required.
Spaceboxes, Utrecht, 2004. Architecture: Mart de Jong, Spacebox®.

Sandwiches

2.1 Honeycomb structures

Honeycomb structures are perfectly suited to serve as pressure-distributing and stiffening core layers in sandwich panels. Based on the beehive model, the hexagonal form has an infinitely repeatable cell structure and exhibits an ideal relationship between wall surface and volume. This natural principle has already made an impact as an intelligent and material-saving construction method in numerous areas of architecture and design.

In order to fabricate honeycomb structures, strips of metal, paper, or plastic are glued or welded together at regular intervals in hexagonal shapes. Then the facing is attached, producing hollow internal spaces that have an **acoustic and thermal insulating effect**. Fine tubules can also be used to create a stable middle layer.[37, 38]

However, core cells that are sealed and rigid do not always represent an advantage. In aircraft construction, for example, it is important for the honeycomb structure to be air permeable, as condensation occurs in the individual air chambers due to differences in atmospheric pressure and temperature. The result can be corrosion. To tackle this adverse phenomenon, a collaboration between Airbus and the Institute of Aircraft Design at the University of Stuttgart developed a honeycomb material resembling an origami structure that is folded out of a single "sheet" of material. The geometry of the honeycomb filters out moisture like a drainage system and the panel core remains ventilated thanks to the continuous hollow space. Furthermore, the major benefit of this

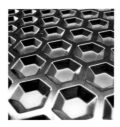

39 — Honeycomb structures can also be drawn directly from sheet metal or board material via forming. If two of these 3D sheets are precisely sandwiched together and covered with facings, the large contact surface available for bonding results in exceptional bending and buckling resistance at a low overall weight. The load-bearing properties are comparable with those of spatial framework construction.

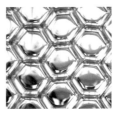

40 — Composite material made of aluminum honeycomb and glass sandwich plates.

folded structure is its formability. Even cylindrical cross sections could be entirely reinforced using this honeycomb structure—something that is geometrically impossible with conventional hexagonal honeycombs.[41]

Finished sandwich panels can also be bent to a certain degree. The bending radius depends on the material and panel thickness. Cutouts are generally unproblematic as the stiffness of the homogenous structure even makes it possible for large holes to be bridged. Panels that come direct from the factory with brackets fitted into the core can be joined together or attached to existing walls, floors, or ceilings. Entire partition systems can thus be prefabricated out of lightweight honeycomb elements. Electricity and network cables for lighting or monitors can also be incorporated within the wall elements. Thanks to their low overall weight, the elements are light and easy to handle during construction.[42, 43]

Apart from their stability, it is the high visual quality of honeycomb sandwiches that makes them appealing to designers. If the exterior layers are designed to be **transparent** or **translucent**, the panels create a pixel effect on movements and objects when illuminated from behind. Honeycomb panels that are utilized for their visual effects in furniture design or interior design are available in clear, matte, or colored versions. One particular challenge is to make the bond between the inner honeycomb core and the facing as invisible as possible. The edges also require special attention because the open sections of the honeycomb structure are visible here. They can be sealed with resin or covered with a profile or strip of material.[47-51]

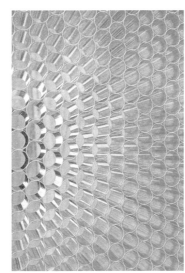

37 — Honeycomb structure made of stainless steel sheet.

38 — UV-stabilized tubular honeycomb core with glass facing, suitable for both exterior glazing and interior applications.

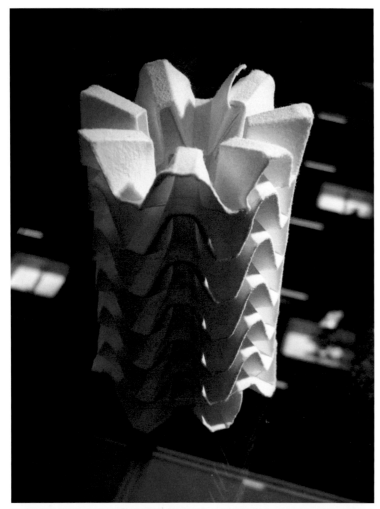

42 — Exhibition furniture: <u>polypropylene sandwich panel</u> bent and then fixed by welding it together with plastic.
Design: Formade, Berlin.

43 — Variable wall system in lightweight design. Sandwich elements with paper cores and MDF exterior layers are joined together with connectors to form wall surfaces—no tools required.

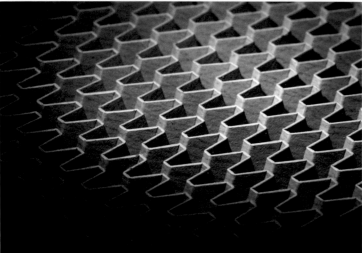

41 — Apart from being able to aerate, the major benefit of a folded honeycomb structure is its formability—even cylindrical bodies can be produced as sandwich cores. The origami-like honeycomb structure can be manufactured off the roll at low cost and can be folded from various materials such as paper, plastic, and metal.
Development: Institute of Aircraft Design (IFB), University of Stuttgart.

44 — "A single idea can transform nothing into something." True to the philosophy of their client—a creative agency called Nothing—the designers Alrik Koudenburg and Joost van Bleiswijk created a remarkable office environment from simple low-cost cardboard honeycomb. 500 m² of cardboard honeycomb panels with a thickness of 15 mm were cut into 1,500 parts using <u>CNC technology</u>. These parts were then simply fitted together like a 3D jigsaw puzzle without any screws or glue. The material has a distinct process-like character and looks like a gigantic model. The detailing is simple and all the raw edges are left open. The designers used an essentially banal material to create an interesting spatial configuration with its own aesthetic.
Creativity Agency Nothing, Amsterdam, 2009. Design & production: Alrik Koudenburg, Joost van Bleiswijk.

45 — Stable paper sandwich elements can be used to build furniture, entire wall structures, or even houses. The core and facing consist of paper impregnated with synthetic resin. Using a special process, <u>cellulose</u> is transformed under pressure and high temperatures into a weatherproof structure. The paper honeycomb cores are available in waterproof and fireproof versions. The sandwich composite is available in widths of 1.5 meters and customizable lengths. An entire house has been developed from the paper panels as a prototype for emergency accommodation in crisis zones. The Universal House requires just one tree's worth of material, and the basic version costs around $ 5,000.
Universal House, 2008. Architecture: Prof. Dirk Donath, Bauhaus-Universität Weimar. Engineer: Gerd Niemöller.

Sandwiches – Honeycomb structures

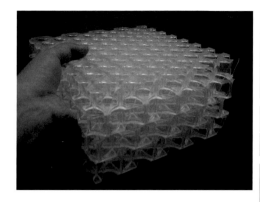

46 — In his pavilion for Bruges, Toyo Ito tested the load-bearing relationship between a honeycomb core and the stiffening facing by minimizing the materials as far as possible. Focusing initially on the honeycomb structures built from aluminum strips, experiments were conducted on models to explore the possibilities for reinforcing the structure with partially attached elliptical patches. The design impact on the pavilion's appearance was investigated on every scale, from paper models to a lifesize mock-up in the steel workshop. In the final construction, a honeycomb structure measuring 12.5 cm in depth was overlaid with 3 mm thick aluminum plates that were calculated to provide sufficient reinforcement and form a load-bearing composite structure.

The entire construction was covered in a skin of transparent polycarbonate panels for protection against the weather. The result is an extremely light, semi-transparent shell of high aesthetic appeal with surfaces that resemble the patterns of traditional Belgian lacework.

Brugge Pavilion, Belgium, 2002. Architecture: Toyo Ito & Associates, Tokyo. Engineers: Structural Design Office Oak. Inc.

Sandwiches – Honeycomb structures

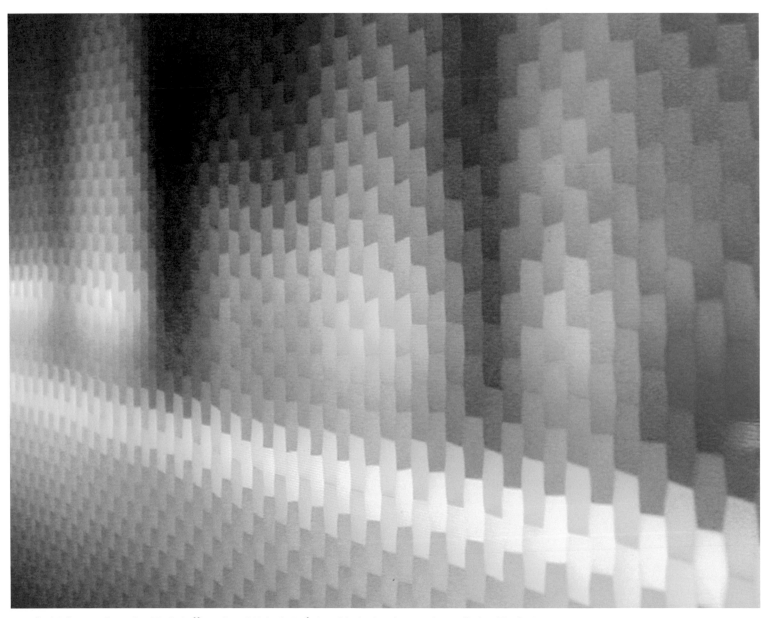

47 —Backlit honeycomb panels with pixel effect, glass cloth laminate facing with aluminum honeycomb core. Design: Flux Design.

48 — Visual effect created by honeycomb glass panels with custom-colored orange tubular core.
Illinois Institute of Technology (IIT), 2003. Architecture: OMA, Rotterdam.

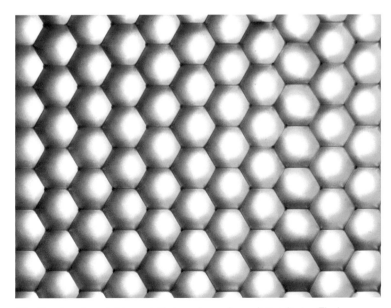

49 — Translucent sandwich panels that can be used as a digital display. The honeycomb core is fitted with LEDs that are controlled by a special software and can show pictures and films.

50 — Edge sealed with resin.

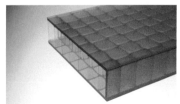

51 — A honeycomb inlay made of clear PET plastic is bonded with acrylic glass facing. The edges are closed with the same facing material, and permanently bonded with transparent adhesive.

Sandwiches – Honeycomb structures

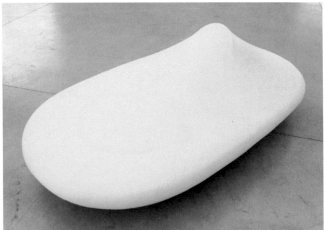

52 — This sofa conceals its true character under a highly stretchable 3D spacer fabric. At first sight it appears merely as a simple oval. But hidden interior mechanisms can raise supports to change the overall shape into a three-dimensional seating object. The design makes use of the maximum elasticity that characterizes the multilayered stretch jersey material. The fabric has a sandwich-like structure consisting of a 2-3 mm core made of elastic polyurethane fiber with textile facings. Because of its soft, light-weight and ventilatory properties it is highly suited for seating applications. The sofa was designed for Tokyo Fiber '09 – Senseware exhibition.
Moshi-moshi, Tokyo, 2009. Design: Antonio Citterio.

Sandwiches – Soft Sandwiches

2.2 Soft Sandwiches

If the honeycomb is made using not rigid but elastic material, it can be deformed in dynamic ways. Honeycomb made of thermoplastic elastomer has a **"memory effect"** that makes the material instantly spring back to its original shape when no longer under pressure. Moreover, the flexible plastic facing creates an air cushion that supports the shock-absorbing effect of the honeycomb geometry.[53]

56 — The Lounge Landscape consists of 3D polyester spacer fabric with GRP facing on both sides. The wave-like surface was computer-generated using mathematical equations that represent the logic inherent within the material and that can be manipulated to create specific morphologies. Material, statics, and ergonomics thus become the decisive criteria in the design process. The surfaces of the resulting lounge landscape can be used in various ways for sitting, reclining or lying down. Lounge Landscape, 2007. Development & design: Offenbach Academy of Art and Design, Prof. Achim Menges.

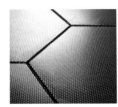

53 — Soft sandwiches provide a cushioning underlayer in seating and beds. In resilient formats, they can also be used as floor covering for trade fairs, gymnastics halls, or spa areas. Heat-sealed hexagonal tiles can be deployed as a quick solution for laying large areas of modular flooring. Thanks to the flexible cell structure, the material is even resistant to stiletto heels.

Sandwich structures made of woven fabric material are increasingly attracting the attention of designers. **"3D spacer fabrics"** made of elastic synthetic fiber are based on two layers of textile facing that are spatially interwoven. Thanks to the configuration of their weave and alignment, the vertically positioned fibers within the core ensure outstanding pressure distribution and exceptional air and moisture permeability, making the material ideal for serving as cushioning for seating and mattresses.[52, 54, 55]

If the 3D textile is woven entirely from **glass fiber**, the capillary action of the fine fibers can be used to harden the material into a solid panel. The soft textile is first shaped and then impregnated with synthetic resin. The capillaries absorb the resin and harden once fully saturated and expanded. The result is a dimensionally accurate, integral sandwich structure with low weight and high stability. The material is completely corrosion-proof and will not delaminate—in other words, the facing will not detach. This is a major benefit, particularly in wet or damp environments exposed to spray.[57]

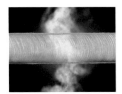

54 — Air and moisture-permeable mattress made of 3D braided fabric.

55 — Spacer fabric made of polyester.

The construction industry also uses textile sandwiches as hollow-body systems. When the internal space is filled with either air, solids, or hardening masses, the layers of facing are kept at an exact distance from one another due to the standardized length of the connecting threads. With the outer layers fixed in this way,

57 — Three-dimensional fabric made of glass fibers that soaks up liquid resin through its capillarity and hardens into a stable slab.

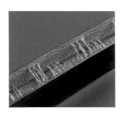

58 — Double-walled fabrics can be filled with sand or water to create noise-protection walls or explosion protection.

the material can be used as lost formwork for concrete.[58]

These "double-walled fabrics" can even be used for **noise-protection walls** made of textile—the hollow space is filled with sound-absorbing sand. Meanwhile, transportable elements filled with water can serve as mobile explosion protection against attacks at major events. The walls of water impede the force of a detonation and prevent the scattering of splinters and pieces of metal.

Pneumatic constructions also utilize the principle of a predetermined flexible shell. The inflated form is stabilized by threads on the inside. Manufacturing technology allows the fabric layers to be held up to a meter apart with a maximum of 110,000 thread connections per square meter.

59 — Also in regard to its overall shape, the vision of a bridge entirely cast of hollow aluminum spheres is reminiscent of bone structures.
Development: University of Bath – Department of Architecture and Civil Engineering, Dr. Chris Williams, Emma Nsgube.

3.0 Foams

In nature, foam-like structures occur in many different forms. They prove effective wherever high stability is required at low weight—like in bone structures, for example. The inside of a bone has a porous structure characterized by its maximized surface area and minimized weight. Countless pores make the material extremely light, while the web of bone tissue distributes and transfers loads with optimum efficiency.

Today, this lightweight construction principle inspired by nature has been translated into technical applications on numerous levels. In automobile construction, **aluminum foams** are used as shock-absorbing **sandwich elements** or as reinforcing cores for hollow sections. This highly energy absorbent material is also deployed in walls as protection against explosions and bullets. Easy to process with sawing or milling, metal foam is also completely recyclable. Its density is just 10 % of the original material.[60]

Thanks to its porous structure, aluminum foam is sound-absorbing and can offer a visually interesting alternative to conventional **acoustic ceilings**.

The large surface area of the material also makes it ideal for use in climate-control elements. With copper or stainless-steel pipes embedded inside, the non-flammable metal panels can even serve as "dry sprinklers" that are cooled with water in the event of fire. Heat is immediately abstracted by the large surface area, thereby protecting structural elements within the building. This

Foams

makes it possible to avoid the massive water damage caused by standard sprinklers. In the reverse case, the material can also be used for heat-distributing elements.

The surface can be manufactured either with a natural finish, in metallic tones or in RAL colors.[66]

Another variety of foam is the **advanced pore morphology** (APM) foam developed at the Fraunhofer Institute for Applied Materials Research. Its properties can be customized with even greater accuracy than pure foam panels because the "pearl" size and wall thickness are precisely adjustable to individual structural requirements. The foam spheres can be made of many different metals including stainless steel, titanium, gold, and silver. Larger, geometrically complex elements can be manufactured by bonding individual spheres together with resins or sintering them in a kiln.[61]

Because of their fine pore structure, foams are not only robust, but also have exceptional insulating properties. Innumerable polymer-based foam products such as foamed polyurethane and polystyrene are standard materials in the construction industry, and have been for decades. But glass and clay can also be expanded into porous structures. **Expanded clay** and **expanded glass** are processed into granules that can be poured, providing exceptional thermal and acoustic insulation, and are non-flammable, solvent-free, and weather-resistant. Different grain sizes can be used as additives for lightweight concrete or acoustic plaster. As cement-bonded or resin-bonded insulation or leveling material, they are suitable for load-bearing floors. Expanded clay gives building elements a balanced climate system. The ceramic granules permeated with air pores ensure optimum thermal insulation and thermal storage at the same time.[62, 65]

60 — Hollow-profile reinforced with aluminum foam.

61 — APM foam sphere structures.

From an ecological standpoint, a particularly interesting development in lightweight construction is **wood foam.**

The starting point is the fact that the global wood-processing industry generates 200 million cubic meters of wood shavings and sawdust every year. But the possibilities for selling or processing this byproduct are limited, which is why wood foam was developed as a recycling material.

Here, shavings and sawdust are treated according to an ancient method. Water and starch are added to create a wood paste rather like bread dough. The resulting mass is expanded with the help of yeasts and bacteria and then dried out. What emerges is an

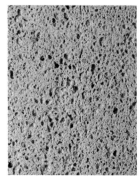

62 — Expanded clay granule.

63 — Wood foam.

64 — Lightweight sandwich panel with wood foam granules.
Development: Johannes Ebner, FH Lippe, Höxter.

65 — Expanded glass granule in a close-up and in bulk.

entirely new kind of wood material that can be processed into lightweight sandwich construction elements by enclosing it between layers of facing either as a solid core or as granules.

Weighing between 250 and 300 kg/m³, wood foam is exceptionally lightweight and contains no glue. It has outstanding acoustic properties and can be sanded, drilled, sawn, or screwed. It is also incredibly simple to recycle—it can be mechanically shredded and watered down into a pulp that is reprocessed into combustible pellets for wood-burning heating systems.[63, 64]
— **"Foam materials" page 41**

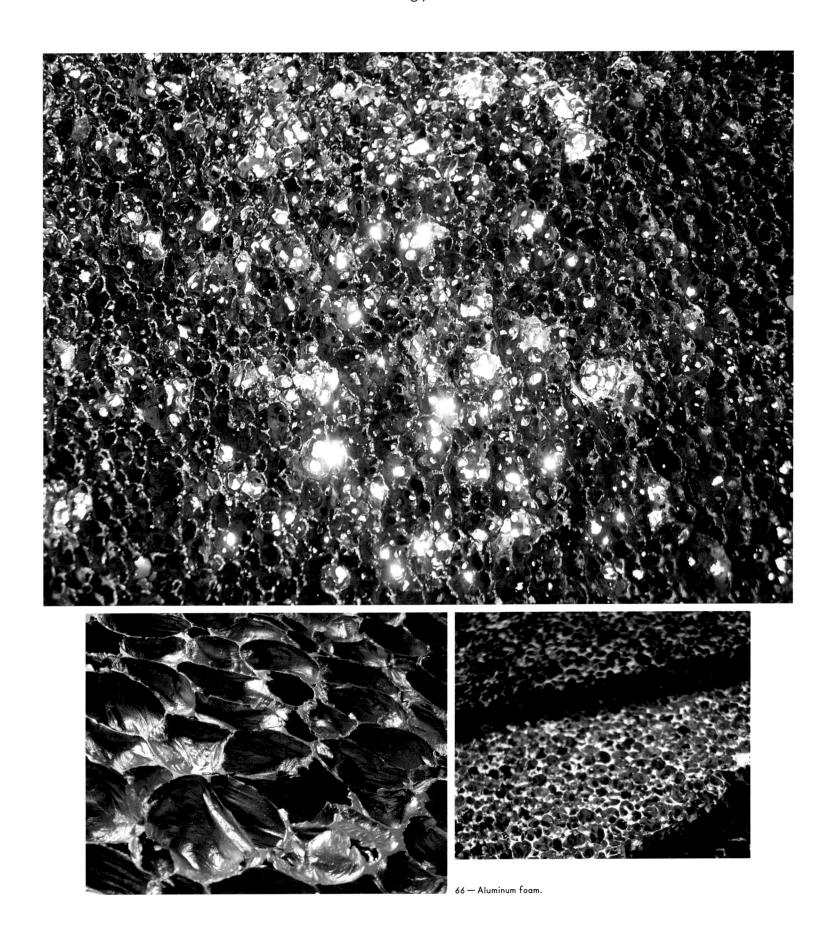

66 — Aluminum foam.

Foams

Glossary

Fiber-reinforced polymers (FRPs)

FRPs are individually designed for a specific purpose. Material composition and fiber orientation are tailored to the type of load.

They consist of two components—the fibers and the surrounding matrix. The matrix serves to fix and protect the fibers from external and mechanical influences. It also transmits shear forces. The fibers transmit the tensile forces.

Fibers
Glass fiber

Has extremely good chemical resistance and is thermally insulating and fireproof. Its mechanical properties are modest. Glass fiber is relatively cost-efficient.

Carbon fiber

Has outstanding mechanical properties. Its tensile strength is 15 times greater than steel but it is relatively cost-intensive. Suitable for high-performance structural elements.

The black carbon fibers are manufactured from the petroleum derivative PAN (polyacrylonitrile) that is carbonized via pyrolysis ("charring" under oxygen-free conditions) at approx. 1,500°C.

Polymer fiber

Aramid fiber (aromatic polyamide fiber; brand names include Kevlar, Twaron, and Nomex) is extremely heat resistant, impact resistant, and energy absorbing. Applications include bulletproof vests, wall armoring, and fireproof textiles.

Polyethylene fiber (brand names include Spectra and Dyneema) has extremely low density and even greater specific strength than aramid fiber. It is also used for enhancing the impact resistance of armoring, or is deployed as a robust top layer on heavy-duty surfaces.

Natural fiber

Made from plants. Flax, hemp, jute, sisal, and cotton are suitable for fiber composites.

Basalt fiber

Derived from basalt (an igneous rock). In terms of quality, it ranks between glass and carbon fiber but is lower-cost than carbon, making it suitable for lightweight constructions on a mass scale. It has high chemical resistance and heat resistance to approx. 800°C. The material is recyclable.

Matrix
Thermosetting plastics

No longer plastically deformable once they have cured. These resin materials include polyester resin, epoxy resin and vinylester resin. Thermosetting plastics are not recyclable but can be used as fuel (incineration).

Thermoplastics

Can be plastically formed at high temperatures but have lower strength than thermosetting plastics. They can be melted down for recycling. Materials include polypropylene (PP) and polyethylene (PE). Most of the biopolymers based on starch or polylactic acid (PLA) are also thermoplastics.
— see page 13

Manufacturing processes for fiber-reinforced plastic (FRP) elements

For the production of formed elements, different manufacturing processes are available. The necessary reinforcing fibers are inserted one layer at a time into a negative mold and then impregnated with resin. The first layer in the mold—the "gelcoat"—is the outermost layer of resin on the finished element. It is fiber-free and determines the surface quality. This is followed by several layers of the reinforcing fiber in the form of mats which are impregnated with the binding resin.

Compression process

Fiber mats are impregnated with resin and then pressed into shape. The pressure helps to distribute the resin and saturate the fiber. Common process for medium and high-volume production.

Hand lay-up process

Fiber mats are placed in a mold in layers and impregnated with resin. Air is removed by rolling out each layer. The material cures at room temperature. For prototypes and short production runs or geometrically complex parts.

Fiber spray-up process

The resin and chopped glass fiber are sprayed together into the mold and the air is then rolled out. The chopped fibers assume a non-directional arrangement in the mold. The finished material attains only a relatively moderate level of strength.

Injection or infusion process

The dry fiber product is placed in a closed mold. The resin is then injected into the fixed fiber material under high pressure—or a vacuum is created and the resin is sucked in. The injection process makes it possible to fabricate composites with high fiber content, thereby enabling good strength with constantly reproducible quality.

— see page 14

Sandwiches

Sandwich material consists of two layers of facing with a core material in between. The components act together to create a stable and lightweight material. There are innumerable combinations on the market that offer particular characteristics (thickness, insulation, format, visual appearance). Sandwich cores are usually made of wood, paper, metal, or plastic. The facing is made of metal, plastic, wood, or paper and serves to stiffen the overall composite. The characteristics of the material are determined by the different core structures.

Pore structures

Materials with low density (foams, lightwood) and good insulating properties.

Honeycomb structures

Hexagonal honeycombs are also commonly found in nature as an efficient method for creating spatial structures. Honeycomb cores are excellent at absorbing forces perpendicular to the panel.

Tube structures

Fine tubular sections are bonded together and cut into sheets. Used for optical purposes or as light-transmitting inserts in translucent thermal insulation.

Three-dimensionally formed structures

Pillow plates and corrugated plates allow air, gas or liquids to flow through the sandwich interior and have a stiffening effect due to their three-dimensional core structure.

— see page 26

Foam materials

Synthetic foam

Polymers are expanded by inserting gas, foaming agent, or air during the manufacturing process. Depending on the particular chemical composition, the resulting material can contain large volumes of air and can either be rigid or elastic. Polyurethane and polystyrene are among the most frequently used synthetic foams in the construction industry and are primarily used for insulating purposes.

Metal foam (mostly aluminum)

Die-casting process: First, a negative mold is made of polymer granules. Then an aluminum melt is infiltrated, the material is heated up, and the polymer melts away to leave the open-celled aluminum foam structure.

Foaming process: An aluminum alloy is prepared in the form of a powder mixture and enriched with a gas-releasing foaming agent. On further heating, the foaming agent is released to produce a highly porous metallic material with an evenly patterned close-celled structure.

Glass foam

Expanded glass is made of collected recycling glass, which is first ground into a powder before being mixed with water along with binder and expanding agents. It is then formed into round granules and is finally "expanded" at approx. 900°C to produce an extremely stable and lightweight glass granulate with microscopic air chambers in the interior.

Clay foam

The basic product for the manufacturing of expanded clay is pure Jurassic clay that is formed into granules and fired at around 1,200°C. This causes the organic components of the clay to combust and the granules expand.

Wood foam

Wood shavings and sawdust are transformed into a wood dough by adding water and starch. This mass is expanded with the help of yeasts and bacteria and then dried. The result is an entirely new type of wood material that can be processed into lightweight sandwich construction elements where it is enclosed between layers of facing, either as the solid core panel or as granules.

Ceramic foam

An open-celled polyurethane foam is impregnated with ceramic slurry. When heated in a kiln, the polymer combusts to leave the foam-like ceramic structure intact. Ceramic foam is heat-resistant to temperatures over 1,000°C and is used for filtering and insulation purposes.

— see page 38

B
42 — 113

Material follows Form

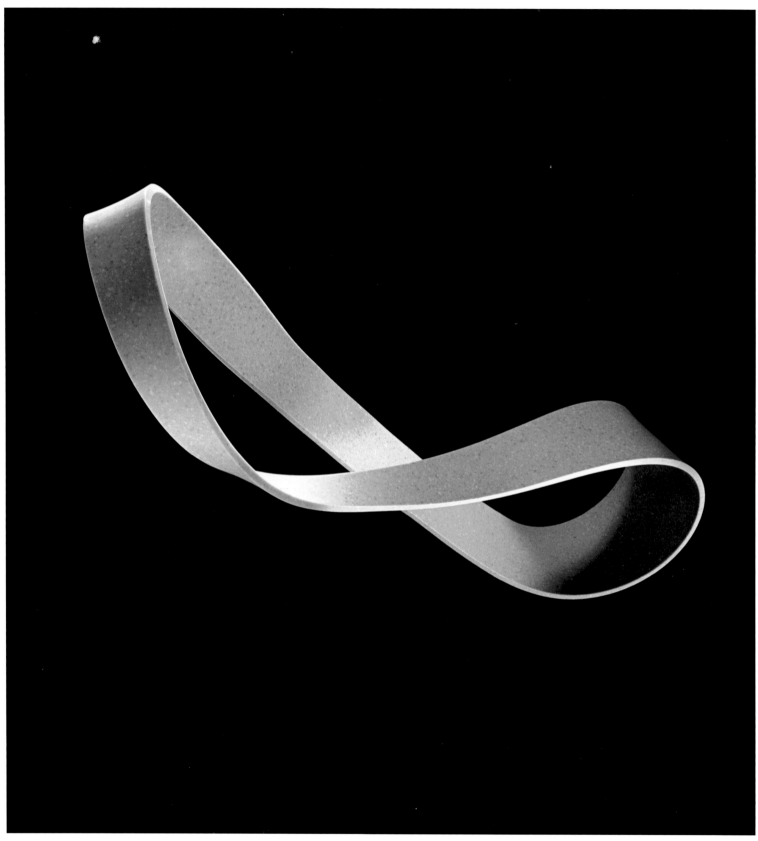

1 — Free-formed solid surface material.

The overall material

0.0 The overall material

Spaces that appear to be made from a single fluid piece are a recurring motif in contemporary architecture. Walls, floors, ceilings, and furniture merge into a three-dimensional continuum. But what are the most suitable materials and technologies for producing this effect?

Material processing is a steadily expanding field. The technologies used to process materials are constantly advancing, making it possible to manufacture increasingly complex shapes. But the technical properties of specific materials still need to be taken into consideration here to ensure that no undue strains, tensions, or cracks are allowed to arise. Casting, forming, and machining are among the most important methods in the generation of free-formed surfaces.

In order to manage the geometric challenges of free-formed surfaces, computer-based planning tools **(CAD: Computer-aided Design)** and production technology **(CAM: Computer-aided Manufacturing)** have become essential components in the work of architects and engineers. Programmable scripts—computational tools that are customized for each new project—allow geometric forms to be described in mathematical terms and to be divided up into individual parts.

This means that even shapes with multiple curves can be broken down into elements that are technically feasible to manufacture. The information required for production is generated within the program and relayed directly to the processing site. Computer-aided tools such as **CNC milling machines** translate the specifications into to the cutting of the material. With these developments, the tasks of process and communication management have become central to the ways in which architecture is created.

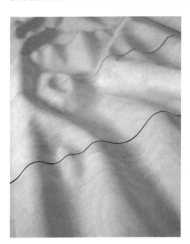

2 — Three-dimensionally formed plywood panels.

Suitable materials for creating continuous surfaces include formable or monocast materials and as coatings applied to pre-formed elements.

With an appropriately shaped formwork, the structural shell of a free-formed building can be created from a single cast of **concrete**. Plastic elements are also viable for producing three-dimensionally curved surfaces. **Glass-fiber-reinforced plastic** is

3 — Thermoformed glass pane.

4 — Fabric-formed concrete.

5 — Fluid-formed stainless steel sheet.

high-quality in appearance and can be manufactured as prefabricated elements with extremely large dimensions.[8] Synthetic-based **solid-surface materials** are available in sheets that can be joined together to form homogenous surfaces. The joints are sealed with the same material and then sanded down until no transitions are visible.

Coverings and **coatings** are applied as the uppermost material layer to pre-formed surfaces. Apart from their functional and protective role, coatings such as mineral plaster have been a significant factor in determining the appearance of buildings for centuries. They cover the vertical surfaces of a structure, adhering to materials such as masonry, concrete, and even insulation.

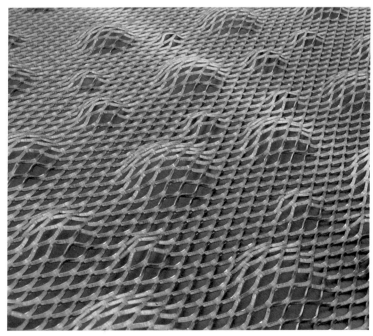

6 — Punctually deformed expanded copper.

The overall material

7 — A clothing store as soft as the clothes themselves. The architects used thin strips of white PVC that, spanned across steel bars, form the free-flowing shelves and counters of this fashion store. Behind the organic forms of the PVC surfaces, fluorescents make the surface glow from inside, evenly illuminating the space.
United Bamboo Store, Tokyo, 2003.
Architecture: Acconci Studio, New York.

The overall material

8 — The perfectly high-gloss-lacquered, smooth surfaces of the glass-fiber-reinforced plastic were prefabricated as only 6 mm thick modules and attached to a substructure on site. The negative forms required to produce the plastic panels were made directly from the architects' 3D digital data using a five-axle CNC milling machine. For transport, the three-dimensional elements were divided into up to 7 m² segments. They serve as display surfaces, seating furniture and counters.
Little Red Riding Hood, Berlin, 2004. Architecture: Corneille Uedingslohmann Architekten, Cologne.

The overall material

The plaster adapts to the geometry of the underlying structure and, in doing so, levels out unevennesses. Nowadays, buildings can also be coated with liquid plastics whose technical properties make them capable of covering even horizontal surfaces.[17]

Stretched foils and fabrics are another alternative for creating seamless curved forms. Welded or stitched together to produce continuous surfaces, the **membranes** are equally suitable for indoor and outdoor applications such as large roof canopies. However, membrane materials are suitable only for tensile applications. Cables, frames, or pneumatic air pressure tighten the materials into stable concave or convex geometries.[7, 18]

9 — Three-dimensionally shaped interior made from thermoformed solid surface material, Puerta America Hotel room, Madrid, 2005. Architecture: Zaha Hadid Architects, London.

1.0 Solidified

1.1 Cast

Concrete

Liquid stone—this synonym for concrete expresses the aesthetic fascination of poured artificial stone. Starting off as a flowing substance that can be formed into any amorphous shape, it hardens to become a symbol of strength and durability.

In order to produce a closed surface with as few pores as possible, care must be taken to employ the right mixing and production techniques for the material. The kind of additives and grain size depend on the structural and visual requirements. To prevent air bubbles, concrete must be deaerated by vibration equipment before it cures.

However, when it comes to highly complex shapes that require dense reinforcement, concrete can no longer be compacted using conventional vibration equipment because the tools cannot reach between the tight reinforcing mesh. This is where new material technologies come into play—like **self-compacting concrete**, for example. It has excellent flow characteristics and deaerates under the force of its own weight. This is achieved by adding a plastic-based liquefier and avoiding coarse-grained additives. Self-compacting concrete enables surfaces of exposed concrete to be produced with extremely smooth and non-porous results.

10 — Fabric-formed concrete used for embankment stabilization. Allegheny Reservoir, New York, 1967.

11 — Fabric-formed concrete elements reflect the moment distribution, making them a highly suitable option for efficient structural designs.

For thin-walled and delicate building components, high-performance concretes based on **ultrafine cement** and a special binder are a good solution. These are extremely resistant to abrasion, frost, and de-icing salt, and they absorb almost no dirt because of their high surface density. Furthermore, their excellent stability means that even the most intricate details and edges can be made fracture resistant.[16, 19]

But the design outcome can be influenced by more than just the particular composition of the material. The construction and type of the casting mold—in this case the formwork—is also significant.

12 — Fabric membranes can also be used as formwork walls when stretched in special frames. Spacers give the surface a pillow-like structure which can take on a fine fabric texture, depending on the textiles used.
Fabric-formed concrete. Development: C.A.S.T., University of Manitoba, Canada.

With complex geometries, the arrangement of the formwork panels is a significant challenge and needs to be factored into the overall planning at an early stage. The size and thickness of the chosen panels influence the geometry of the structure. Even double-curved surfaces can be produced using conventional formwork. The panels are bent and fixed onto a substructure on site, taking their maximum ductility into account.[15]

Another way of building free-form surfaces with concrete is to use fabrics as formwork. Fabric-formed concrete has been deployed for the structural stabilization of embankments and trenches since the 1960s.[10]

Here, stiff formwork panels are replaced by a flexible **membrane** which deflects according to the laws of gravity when the concrete is poured. C.A.S.T.—the Centre for Architectural Structures and Technology at the University of Manitoba's Faculty of Architecture—has focused on using this principle in structural applications. The forms produced as the fabric is tensioned by the freshly poured concrete are consistent with the moment distribution and thus assume a structurally efficient shape. In order to fabricate particularly thin cross sections, the concrete can be reinforced with **glass or carbon fiber** instead of steel bars.

Furthermore, the fabric acts as a drainage system during the concreting process, filtering out excess air and water and enabling the concrete surface to cure quickly and permanently. The most frequently used materials are polyethylene or polypropylene-based permeable fabric membranes that are available in strips up to 100 meters long and can be reused on numerous occasions as the concrete does not stick to them. Thus there is no need for the lubricants required in conventional formwork construction. The fabrics are between 100 and 300 times lighter than formwork panels at just one tenth of the price. So apart from saving resources, this development also saves money.

As concrete is one of the most commonly used building materials worldwide, this technology could have a particularly significant impact in simplifying the construction process in economically underdeveloped regions.[11, 12]

Solid surface

Solid surface materials offer a wealth of possibilities for designing freeform shapes and continuous surfaces. They are available in various compositions and colors.[16] Their main ingredients are mineral powders and color pigments. The binder matrix comes in the form of **acrylic or polyester-based resins** which are dyed through with pigments. This means that the velvety, non-porous surface can be refinished and restored over and over again.

The material is produced in sheets or prefabricated elements. Large continuous surfaces can be created by gluing individual sheets together to form a seamless whole. Once the sheets have been bonded together using a compound of the same material, the joints are sanded until the transitions are no longer visible.

13 — Solid surface materials in various colors.

Curved surfaces and three-dimensional objects such as washbasins can also be produced by thermoforming the material on prefabricated plywood or metal templates. While initially reserved for interior applications, the material has now started being utilized for façades. Its UV resistance is particularly good with lighter colors.[20]

Free-form structures can be cast from solid surface materials using a two-component system in which water-based solvent-free acrylic resin is combined with mineral powder. The material is non-toxic, odorless, and will not contract.
— **"Solid surface" page 112**

14 — The solid surface is formed until it looks like a colossal piece of chewing gum being pulled though a glass wall.
Corian Design Studio, Philadelphia, 2009. Architecture: Harry Allan, New York.

Solidified – Cast

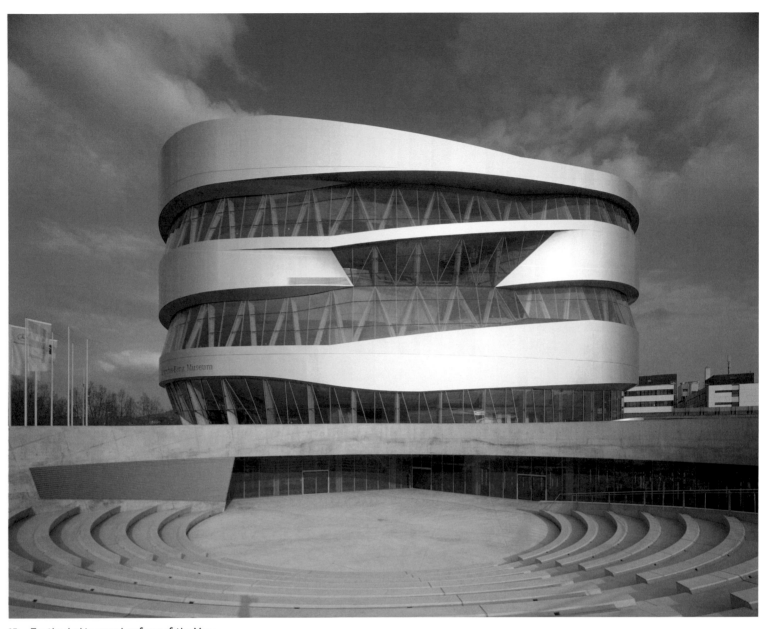

15 — For the double-curved surfaces of the Mercedes Benz Museum in Stuttgart, flat standard panels were fixed into a "pre formwork" that marked out the geometry. Right from the early design phase of the project, the calculations for the curvature of the building were aligned with the calculated elastic deformation of the formwork panels. Using 3D computer modeling, unfolded views for each material were generated that factored in the characteristics of the panels. This made it possible to construct precise surfaces despite the complex, non-standard shapes involved. The positioning of each panel joint was implemented to the exact half-millimeter.
Mercedes Benz Museum, Stuttgart, 2005. Architecture: UN Studio, Amsterdam. Planning of the formwork: designtoproduction, Stuttgart/Zurich.

16 — Walls made of <u>glass-fiber-reinforced concrete</u> just 7 cm thick. The glass fiber was added into the liquid concrete and the mixture was then cast. To reduce the construction time, the walls were prefabricated while the roof was concreted on site. The countless openings in the structure were produced using plywood and expanded polystyrol blocks in the formwork.
Shin Yatsushiro Monument, Yatsushiro, Japan, 2004.
Architecture: Kumiko Inui, Tokyo.

17— In order to give a homogenous visual appearance to all the surfaces of the building, the Dupli.Casa villa designed by Jürgen Mayer H. Architects was covered with functional material layers that create an overall impression of unity. All the vertical surfaces on the building were treated with a fine-grained silicate plaster. Horizontal, overhanging, and inclined surfaces with greater exposure to rainwater and moisture were covered with a white polyurethane spray coating that is waterproof and easy to clean. Even the floor surface of the patio is part of the overall look with its white amorphous shape. Made of white rubber granulate, it creates a seamless transition from the house to the garden. In order to achieve the consistent curves of the façade, the mineral foam of the exterior insulation and finishing system (EIFS) was first sawn into the desired shape, then stuck into place, and finally rasped and sanded down. Dupli.Casa villa near Ludwigsburg, Germany, 2005. Architecture: Jürgen Mayer H. Architects, Berlin.

18 — Pneumatic membrane construction used as a temporary stage for a jazz festival. The rounded perimeters are produced by a thin steel frame that supports a pneumatic tube measuring one meter in diameter. Stretched over this entire construction is a foil that creates a soft transition between the frame and the surface membrane made of coated PVC fabric.
Tubaloon, Kongsberg Jazz Festival, Norway, 2006. Architecture: Snøhatta AS, Oslo.

19 — The <u>self-compacting high performance concrete</u> is reinforced with steel fibres. The sharp-edged 100 meter long ornamental wall that is made up of individual parts measuring 80 x 80 cm.
Cocoon Club Concrete Wall, Frankfurt, 2004. Architecture & design: 3deluxe, Wiesbaden. Development of concrete elements: Villa Rocca.

Solidified – Cast

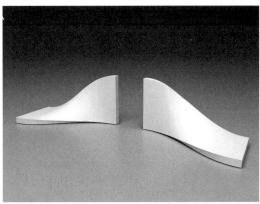

20 — Solid surface panels with a thickness of 6 mm were thermoformed on wooden templates at 200°C. The individual pieces were then glued together to create three-dimensional elements that serve as display surfaces in a luxury shoe store in Rome.
Stuart Weitzman shoe Store, Rome, 2006.
Design: Fabio Novembre, Milan.

Solidified – Cast

1.2 Coated

One effective and low-cost method for producing homogenous surfaces is **coating**. Here, the underlying structure remains the key element in defining the shape to which the coating adapts. Large coherent surfaces can be created in a single step by spraying or spreading on the material.

Unlike conventional concrete which is first poured into a mold and then compacted, **shotcrete** does not require any formwork. Instead, it is directly applied to the surface as a coating. Due to the high air-pressure generated in the spraying process, the material is compacted upon impact and the excess air is instantly expelled.

The process was originally used for stabilizing rock faces in tunnel and road construction. It is an extremely good method for concreting continuous, curved volumes. Depending on the selected grain size, the surface of the untreated material is quite raw after curing.[29, 30]

In order to give existing walls or furnishings a concrete look, a layer of mineral mortar just 1 mm thick can be applied to a backing material. Containing a high proportion of marble sand, the resulting concrete skin is an ideal solution for the flexible and lightweight demands of shop or trade-fair construction.[21]

21 — Millimeter-thin concrete coating for interior design. Standard dimensions of the coated wood panels: 260 x 101 cm.

22 — The reception desk of the Ellington Hotel in Berlin was covered with a real metal coating of brass, then smoothed and polished. Refurbishment of the Ellington Hotel, Berlin, 2007. Architecture: Reuter Schoger Architekten Innenarchitekten, Berlin.

Metal, too, can be sprayed onto substrates such as MDF, wood, or plastic. A liquid metal skin can be deployed to provide a coating on furniture. It is composed of 90% real metal particles and just 10% binding agent. Afterwards it can be polished or sanded to various degrees. The surfaces develop a certain patina over time because real metal pigments are involved. Thanks to the homogenous distribution through spraying, real metal surfaces can be implemented on geometrically complex forms.[22]

Homogeneous metal surfaces of brass, aluminum, or stainless steel that are resilient enough to be walked on or driven over can be made of a resin-bonded coating with metal particles scattered in. The surface roughness can be calibrated to suit the particular application. Because the material is extremely durable and resistant to abrasion, it can even be deployed outdoors.[23]

23 — Resin-bonded aluminum coating for floors.

24 — Pouring a polyurethane coating for a sports track.

25 — Polyurethane spray-coated foam.

Purely **synthetic coatings** can be produced using two-component materials based on epoxy resin or polyurethane. **Epoxy resins** are generally more brittle in structure than polyurethane and only suitable for horizontal surfaces (floors) due to their coating technique. Elastic **polyurethane** can be applied to plasterboard, concrete, metal, or ceramic surfaces. This crack-bridging material—also used for waterproofing roofs or concrete structures, and for fabricating elastic sports floors—can be rolled or sprayed on and is thus capable of being applied to both horizontal and vertical planes. One layer just a few millimeters thick is enough to create a resistant surface. The PU skin is waterproof and yet permeable for vapor diffusion, allowing it to be utilized as a façade coating.[24, 28] When applied to foam, an elastic PU coating can be used as a washable and low-maintenance alternative to fabric upholstery covers. This skin-like surface originates from the healthcare sector where it provides cushions and rests with a moisture-resistant coating. The fascinating contrast between the material's homogenous but sharp-edged appearance and its soft, comfortable surface has made it an increasingly popular choice in furniture design.[25, 26]

One "skin" of a slightly different nature is spray-on fabric. This "textile in a can" consists of fluid cotton fibers that dry upon impact with a surface to form an instant fabric mass. Beyond its technical use in the medical sector as a dressing material, the technology is also enjoying a new lease of life as instant spray-on fashion.[27]

26 — Maarten van Severen first used coated foam in 1999 for his minimalist Blue Bench.

27 — Spray-on fabric.

Solidified – Coated

28 — NL Architects used the crack-bridging polyurethane coating that was originally developed for the
waterproofing of roofs as a façade coating for a
technical facility near Utrecht. The surface needed
to be vandal-proof and easy to clean. The skin was
sprayed onto a concrete-sandstone structure, eliminating the need for details such as gutters and drip
edges. Rainwater finds its own way down the façade
and transforms the surface into an almost artistic
sculpture.
WOS 8, Utrecht, 1998. Architecture: NL Architects.

Solidified – Coated

29 — The triangular structure with a lateral length of 180 meters is totally covered with blue pigmented shotcrete. Numerous window openings as vertical incisions in the partially folded façade reflect the surroundings. An event space with 3,200 seats and an exhibition floor are the main components of this public building.
Forum, Barcelona, 2004, Architecture: Herzog & de Meuron, Basel.

Material follows Form

30 — The form of the skatepark derives from the dynamic movement and trajectory height of the skateboarders. The radii also vary horizontally. In order to produce the complex shapes, the first step was to install a framework that defined the profile along specific lines. This was then treated on site with reinforcements and shotcrete. While initially exhibiting a rather coarse grain, the shotcrete surface was gradually smoothed out with various trowels. Thus the grain of the final surface is so fine that no mechanical disturbance can be felt against the 50 mm wheels of a skateboard.
Skatepark, Stuttgart, 2009. Architecture: Matthias Bauer Associates MBA/S, Stuttgart. Engineers: Knippers Helbig Consulting Engineers, Stuttgart.

2.0 Shaped

2.1 Folded

The technique of folding stabilizes and shapes at the same time and is one of the simplest methods for creating a three-dimensional structure from a two-dimensional material. This can be done on varying scales—from the surface of a panel right up to massive load-bearing structures. The principle can be applied to any type of material from paper to steel.

With the help of a special procedure, sheet metal can be transformed into stable shapes through curvilinear folds. Algorithmic morphology is combined here with digital manufacturing technology to produce three-dimensionally curved surfaces. Thanks to the efficient production process, the technology is referred to as "mass customization." The undulating surfaces are the result of the material's behavior under pressure. Deformation stabilizes the material so that the overall sheet thickness can be reduced. This process can be used to manufacture wall panels, ceiling panels, or column covers.[32]

31 — Origami cylinders can be telescopically extended, whereby the fold becomes a hinge.
Development: University of Oxford, Dr. Zhong You.

The traditional folding technique of origami has been applied by Dr. Zhong You from the University of Oxford to produce extendable cylinders. Here, folds are used not only to stiffen the material but also to serve as hinges. This technique allows elongated cylindrical forms to be collapsed down into small packages. The extended structures are inherently stable and the principle can be implemented with different materials. Possible applications include telescopic arms, transportable liquid containers, or foldable furniture.[31]

If flexible and rigid layers are sandwiched together in a panel and the rigid layer is then removed along certain lines via incision, the flexible layer mutates into a hinge. This creates three-dimensional shapes in relation to the particular material composition and the geometry of the incisions.[33-35]

Another folding principle—the concertina fold—is used by softwall and softseating interior elements manufactured from **polyethylene fabric** and **kraft paper** respectively. Although the modules are no thicker than a book when packed together, they can be

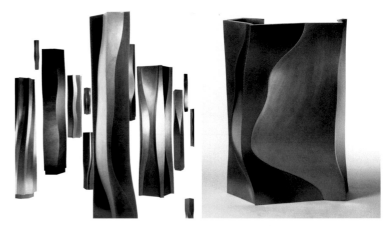

32 — AlgoRhythms: a technology based on algorithmic form-finding principles that folds sheet metal into curved shapes, thus enabling the creation of stable 3D metal structures.
Design & development: Dr. Haresh Lalvani, Milgo/Bufkin, New York.

33 — Foldtex: a flexible sandwich made of a 3 mm thick <u>plywood facing</u> and a tensile fabric. Incisions are cut into the surface via <u>CNC milling</u> to define the edges along which the material can be folded.

34 — The tisch.decken project initiated at the Offenbach Academy of Art and Design is based on Foldtex. The folding is stabilized by a simple tension mechanism, fixing the material into a rigid tabletop. A wax cloth provides the hinge function that enables the folding. The "tablecloth" is self-supporting and mutates into a table when simply placed on two trestles. The plywood laminate can be rolled up for convenient transport.
Foldtex, tisch.decken, 2002. Design: Timm Herok, Suzan D. Cigirac, Sandor Klunker, Germany.

folded out into expansive objects such as curved walls or seating furniture. Magnets on each piece allow different elements to be docked together to create long or circular forms. The freestanding partitions are stable to heights of up to 3 m and can be extended to any length between 2.5 and 6 m, enabling them to be adapted to spatial requirements. The walls are flame-retardant, 100% recyclable, and have a surface that is easy to clean while still retaining an extremely soft and delicate feel.[36]

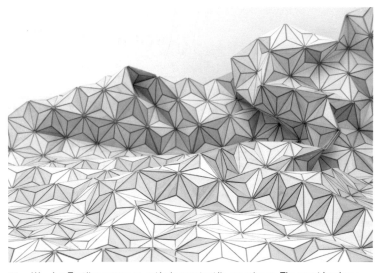

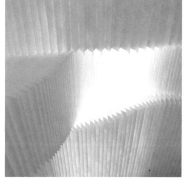
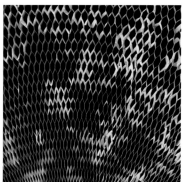

35 — Wooden Textiles convey an entirely new tactile experience. The usual hardness of <u>wood</u> is transformed into a soft flowing surface. It is laser-cut into small tiles and then stuck to one side of a fabric such as silk, lycra, or microfiber. The degree of flexibility depends on the size, shape, and thickness of the wooden segments used. Small tiles result in a fabric-like surface while larger pieces assume an almost structural, architectural quality.
Wooden Textiles. Design: Elisa Strozyk, Germany/United Kingdom.

36 — Paper-light folded elements such as partition walls or seating modules are made of polyethylene or kraft paper that is either a natural brown or dyed black with bamboo charcoal. The edges of the paper honeycomb gradually soften and crush with use (something that the designers intended), lending the surface a unique patina and individual character.
softwall and softblock. Design: molo design, Vancouver.

Shaped – Folded

37 — Voussoir Cloud explores the structural paradigm of pure compression coupled with ultra-light material—<u>wood laminate</u>—that is folded along curved edges for stiffening. In the tradition of Antonio Gaudi, the construction design of the installation was based on computational hanging chain models to evaluate efficient vaulted geometries. Instead of using wedge-shaped vaulted blocks, a special geometry was developed for the lightweight, curved wooden petals that are joined together along their edges. Paper-thin material was folded to create 3D elements that rely on the internal surface tension of the wood and the folded geometry of the flanges to hold their shape. The flanges are under pressure and tend to bulge out. Thus the individual components press against each other across the entire structure, forming a stable system of compressive elements—analogous to classical arch construction. The installation works with 2,300 wooden petals in four different shapes whose geometry and individual curvature were developed with a specially written computer script and cut out using lasers. Voussoir Cloud installation, SCI-Arc Gallery, Los Angeles, 2008. Architecture: IwamotoScott Architecture, San Francisco. Engineering: Happold Engineers. Scripting: Chris Chalmers, John Kim, with consultation by Andrew Kudless.

38 — Ronan and Erwan Bouroullec designed the "clouds" as reorganizable textile structures for walls, ceilings, or room dividers. The system consists of individual modules that can be infinitely combined to free-form shapes. The simple connection and form principle is based on thermocompressed folds in the foamed material, along which it can be shaped as desired. The edges of the modules are connection bars for interlocking the individual modules by simple rubber rings.
Clouds. Design: Ronan and Erwan Bouroullec in collaboration with Kvadrat.

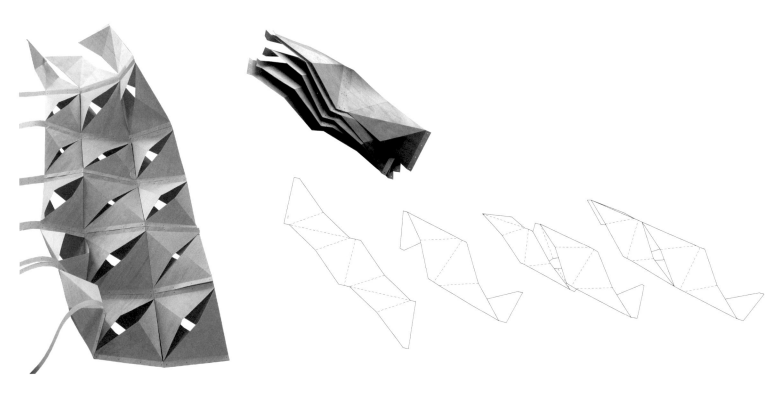

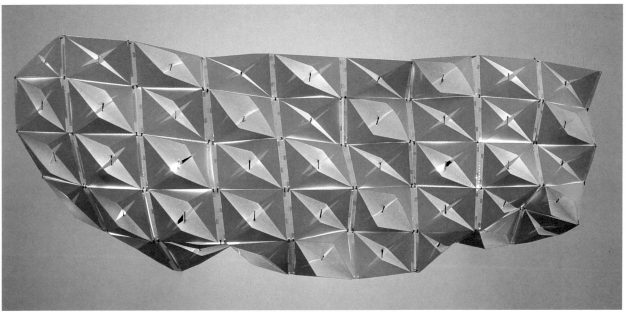

39 — IN-OUT Curtain is a prototype for an adaptable screen that combines modular origami and digital production. The design focuses on creating a flexible and user-responsive system that can change its overall shape both vertically and horizontally. It is designed to function as a transformable room partition or sunblind whose light transmittance can be manually adapted to the respective situation. By means of folding based of the principle of self-similarity, the two-dimensional material turns into a complex, three-dimensional structure. Each module can take on two specific states: IN and OUT — a closed/concave shape, and an open/convex one. The material-inherent tension keeps the elements in their state, yet it is elastic enough to switch from one form to the other when required. When linked together, the individual modules transfer their deformation to all adjacent ones, thus creating ever-new overall shapes.
IN-OUT Curtain, 2005. Architecture: IwamotoScott, San Francisco.

Shaped – Folded

40 — A resilient cladding material was sought for a project on the Welsh coast. The final choice was <u>stainless steel</u>—high in quality but expensive. To save material, the aim was to reduce the sheet thickness as far as possible. The disadvantage of thin sheet metal is the way it dents easily—something that was turned into a deliberate design strategy. Rather than working against the denting, the characteristic was embraced and the surface was first crinkled with custom-made rollers. This stabilized the surface and made it possible to use sheet metal the thickness of a Coke can. For additional stabilization, insulation foam was sprayed onto the back of the surface. The panels overlap vertically so that no joints are visible. The crinkled surface reflects the colors and lighting patterns of the surrounding area in diverse ways, blending harmoniously into the natural environment despite the industrial character of the material.

Aberystwyth Arts Centre, United Kingdom, 2009. Design: Heatherwick Studio, London.

Shaped – Folded

41 — The concrete skeleton of an unfinished hotel was converted to become the company headquarters of a Turkish fashion house. The glass façade had to be kept as thin and transparent as possible to allow the existing structure behind it to show through. For this purpose, panels of insulation glass measuring 335 x 154 cm were developed with a structural X slumped into the outside surface of each panel. This stiffened the large glass surfaces like corrugations in sheet metal, enabling the material thickness to be reduced and eliminating glass frames. The panels were attached to the supporting structure with point fixings. The forming process was carried out in a kiln construction by heating the glass and then lowering it into a negative mold.
Vakko Headquarters, Istanbul, 2009. Architecture: REX, New York. Façade development: Front inc. New York

42 — Almost immaterial and yet extremely stable—a construction made of cold-bent glass. The Pure Glass Bridge spans more than seven meters and won the innovation prize at the Glasstech 2008 Trade Fair in Dusseldorf. The bridge construction was produced by laminating together six 4 mm thick glass sheets with special foil. The resulting shear-resistant glass composite with a total thickness of just 3.7 cm. Side railings glued to the walkway serve to stabilize the construction. The 1.7 metric tons of glass in the bridge can support a load of 7.2 metric tons.
Concept & Design: Institute for Construction and Design, Department 2 (IBK2) at the University of Stuttgart, Prof. Stefan Behling, Ingenieurbüro Engelsmann Peters GmbH, seele sedak GmbH & Co. KG.

2.2 Formed

Panels, sheets, foils, or fabrics can be plastically formed using technologies such as bending or deep drawing. Formed panels exhibit greater stability under load than flat materials of the same thickness.

Unlike with machining processes such as milling and grinding, material is not removed with forming but is shaped into a permanent new form. Material-specific parameters need to be taken into consideration here.

Glass

Relief patterns in ornamental surfaces can be achieved with cast glass that is shaped by rollers. Cast glass is translucent but not transparent.

Flat sheets of float glass can be curved using hot or cold bending processes. In doing so, the surface quality changes and the material loses some visual clarity.

Hot bending requires temperatures in excess of 640°C. The disadvantages of this process are its low dimensional accuracy, the relatively high cost of producing the molds, and the restrictions imposed by the maximum size of the kiln. Sheets up to 5.80 x 2.40 m can be bent to a large radius, with a maximum rise of one meter. Glass surfaces can also be shaped into free-form designs by heating a flat glass sheet until it melts and slumps into a negative mold positioned underneath.[41, 43, 45]

With **cold bending**, several thin and ductile glass sheets are formed by laying them out on a curved mold. The sheets are then laminated together into a material package using a special thermoplastic film that is tougher and stiffer than con-

43 — To produce quilted glass, two sheets that were kiln-formed into congruent shapes are laminated together with fluid <u>polyurethane resin</u> and processed into safety glass panels. The finished surface creates surprising light effects and is available in opaque or transparent versions. Panels measuring up to 2.13 x 3.66 m are available for façades.
Holt Renfrew Flagship Store, Vancouver, 2007. Architecture: Janson Goldstein LLP, New York with Front Inc. New York.

ventional PVB film. Through this method, stresses within the glass are "frozen" into equilibrium.[42]

Wood

The **bending** of solid wood or wood products is not a recent invention. The elastic/plastic potential of plant fiber has been used ever since the first objects were made by weaving rushes and willows. Wood is bent by applying heat, steam, and force to solid wood sections or a stack of veneers.

But a new technique also enables the cold bending of wood. To achieve this, hardwood is pre-compressed against the grain direction using high pressure. This forces the wood cells to fold up and the material acquires an elastic potential. As long as it is kept moist, the wood remains bendable and can be stored in air-tight packaging for months until it is processed. It can be bent into the desired shape by hand or with conventional equipment. Simple drying fixes it into the final position.[48]

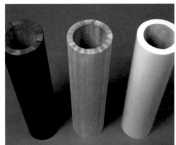

44 — Round wood profile made of compressed semicircular pieces. Development: TU Dresden, Prof. Peer Haller.

In order to improve the structural efficiency of wood, the Institute for Steel and Timber Structures at the Technische Universität Dresden developed a process for manufacturing and forming circular-section timbers that are structurally superior to the conventional rectangular sections made of solid wood. They can be fabricated in lengths and diameters that are not limited by the natural dimensions of timber, and they possess a greater load-bearing capacity. With this type of forming, hardwood or softwood is compacted in presses in a direction perpendicular to the grain. After renewed exposure to heat, the wood is bent, wrapped, or rolled into profiles and then fixed by cooling.[44]

ZipShape is an innovative manufacturing process for bending panels without using any molding equipment. One element consists of two panels that are made with interlocking keys. The keys are geometrically designed so that the two panels only fit together perfectly when bent to the desired curvature. This means that the

Shaped – Formed

45 — 3D computer models were used to fabricate double-curved panes for the Innsbruck Funicular Railway designed by Zaha Hadid Architects. The design objective was to create a homogenous and continuous surface that was also capable of withstanding high technical demands (snow load). The float glass panes measuring up to 1.25 x 3.00 m were formed in a hot bending process as kiln-formed slumped glass. First, a flat glass sheet was placed on a negative mold consisting of a grid of curved steel tubes. By applying heat, the glass settled onto the substructure like a towel, thereby leveling out any imprecisions in the curvature of the steel frame. In a second stage, the float glass pane intended for actual use was slumped onto the sheet below it, again via the hot bending process. The finished glass is secured against breakage with a PU coating that adds a white coloring to the material. To provide the fixings for holding the double-curved elements in place, 2,500 individually-fabricated plastic sections were cut out with a five-axis CNC milling machine. The precise advance calculation of the geometries made it possible for the assembly process to be carried out on site with relatively simple procedures.
Funicular Railway, Innsbruck, 2008. Design: Zaha Hadid Architects, London.

Shaped – Formed

46 — ZipShape: curved panels that are fabricated using just the geometry
of the interlocking keys without form gauges.
Design and development: schindlersalmerón/designtoproduction, Zurich.

47 — FFT (Form Following Texture) material.
3D veneer can also be horizontally warped.

finished form is precisely defined by the panel joints, requiring no
supplementary bracing or forms. The definition of the key geometry is performed with **CAD**, enabling the parameters of material
thickness, key width, key height, and angle to be varied in order to
attain the required curvature. Once defined, the components are
produced via an automatically generated computer code using a
five-axis milling machine and then glued together. It is a particularly good process for manufacturing one-offs or prototypes in furniture and interior design.[46]

Three-dimensionally formed wood surfaces can be fabricated using deep-drawn **veneers**, whereby the appearance of the wood
grain is entirely preserved. The special veneer is produced in
lengths of up to 210 cm, bent into shape with presses, and glued to
the substrate. Possible substrates for the veneers include formed
plywood and materials such as plastics or metal. But not only are
the veneers three-dimensionally bendable, they can also be horizontally distorted so that the grain appears to come from a tree
that grew in a circle rather than a straight line. Thus the wood fibers form a curved pattern. The curve radius is variable and can be
individually adapted to the design. [47, 49]

48 — Cold-bent hardwood, Winery Trellis. 1:1 scale
mock-up of a roof construction made of bent oak.
Design: Gehry Partners, LLP, Los Angeles. Development: Fluted Beams LLC

49 — 3D veneer.

Shaped – Formed

Metal

Metals can be formed by pressure, tension, or bending. A common process for three-dimensional forming is **deep drawing**. This involves applying pressure to the material with a punch, thereby pressing the material into the appropriate die.

In **hydromechanical processes**, the force necessary to press the metal into the negative mold is exerted by water. This "fluid technology" enables the large-scale three-dimensional forming of stainless steel and aluminum sheets into free-form shapes. This novel process has enormous design potential because it can be used to form a variety of objects and motifs, allowing pieces measuring up to 4.5 m² to be processed.[50]

For even larger formats, complex forms, or extremely thick materials, **explosive forming** is a suitable option. This process is conducted underwater. Because no pressing equipment is necessary and the explosives can be individually distributed, it is currently possible to form elements measuring up to 10 x 2 m and with sheet thicknesses up to 60 mm. The only requirement is a negative mold—the conventional punch is replaced by the explosion pressure.

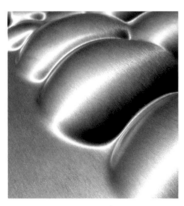

50 — Hydromechanically formed stainless steel sheet (fluid technology).

51 — Vault-structured metal sheets are produced by the deformation of the material under the influence of pressure.

The process of **vault structuring** also makes use of material deformation under the impact of pressure. The effect was first observed by naval scientists in the 1930s. Submarines being tested for stability at great depth returned to the surface with deformations that did not weaken the stability of the hull. On the contrary, they strengthened it.

Unlike the classical linear stiffening of metal sheets using corrugations or flanges, vault structuring works by causing metal sheets to self-fold in three dimensions without using negative molds.

When a critical pressure is reached, the metal sheet—which is partially resting on a supporting structure—springs into three-dimensional honeycomb patterns that lend the surface a high degree of inherent stiffness. This can also be used to stiffen pre-lacquered metal sheets be-

cause no tools touch the surface of the material and the lacquering remains unscratched. The advantages come from savings in material and therefore costs. Sheet-metal coverings on façades or roofs can be fitted using up to 30% less material. Vault-structured metal roofs minimize the drumming effect of rainfall and exhibit low thermal expansion with changes in temperature. Furthermore, the visual glare normally produced by large metal surfaces is softened by the diffusion of the reflected light.[51]
— **"Forming processes for sheet metal" page 112**

2.3 Inflated

Air-supported structures derive their geometry from the contouring of an inflatable shell. The first step here is to transpose the desired shape into a two-dimensional layout cutting pattern. By welding or sewing the individual **sections of membrane** together, a shell is formed that inflates into a spatial structure when internal air pressure is applied. The expansion parameters and the tensile forces of the material must be precisely calculated in advance in order to attain the desired result.

52 — Mobile room system that can be transported in a bag. It consists of polyurethane-coated rip-stop nylon, weighs 12 kg and takes around 10 minutes to inflate. Different sizes provide space for groups of between 3 and 20 people.
Office in a Bucket — OIAB, 2003. Design and development: Inflate, London.

53 — A special textile impregnated with cement is inflated with air pressure to provide emergency accommodation, hardening into permanent concrete when sprayed with water.

For large-volume spaces, the entire structure can be pressurized from within using permanent blowing equipment. Airlocks are then required at the transitions from inside to outside.[58]

But air can also be permanently enclosed within tubes or cushions. Two or three layers of foil are fixed at the edges in a rigid framework. The structure is then brought into final shape and stabilized by the insertion of air. Valves serve to regulate the air supply to the internal hollow spaces. Pneumatic cushions can assume rectangular, rhomboid, or free-form shapes.[52, 54]

54 — Free-standing temporary pavilions as modular pneumatic systems. The inflatable cushion structure is made of tear-resistant, reinforced PVC. "Dome at the Hampton Court", London, 2008 and "Turtle Modular Systems", 2008. Design and development: Inflate, London

Inflatable structures are easy to transport and thus ideal in situations where temporary and quickly erected buildings are needed for emergency accommodation in crisis zones. Developed as a "solid" alternative to fabric tents, the Concrete Canvas Shelter provides inflatable emergency accommodation made of **concrete**. Air and water are the only things required to set it up. The structure itself consists of an inner synthetic membrane and an outer textile layer that is 13 mm thick and impregnated with **cement**. Both layers are inflated together from the inside with an electric ventilator. Once the maximum dimensions have been reached, water is sprayed onto the "concrete cloth" from the outside to harden the cement mixture into a solid shell. The entire structure dries and is ready for use within the space of a day. One unit measuring 54 m² that provides shelter for 15 people can be erected by two people in less than two hours. The outer skin is fireproof, provides thermal insulation, and can even be earthbermed to provide greater insulation and protection against small-arms fire in conflict zones.[53]

— **"Membrane materials for pneumatic constructions" page 113**

Materials suitable for inflation need to be non-rip and airtight—such as coated textiles or foils. At present, the most commonly used material in membrane production is the fluoropolymer foil **ETFE** (ethylene tetrafluoroethylene). The visual clarity of ETFE combined with its UV-resistant, self-cleaning, and flame-retardant characteristics make it suitable for high-quality architectural applications. When processed into a lightweight transparent foil, it offers an alternative to glass in roof structures and has been utilized to this effect by the construction industry since the late 1980s. While its original deployment in greenhouses, swimming facilities, and sports halls was purely functional, architects have recently discovered the material's huge aesthetic potential.

Equally common is **PVC** foil (polyvinyl chloride), which is only suitable for interior or temporary applications due to its low UV resistance. The material is relatively low-cost but not particularly stable and its expansion behavior is highly temperature-dependent. In addition, airtight-coated textiles based on glass fiber, polyester, or fluoropolymer can be used as pneumatic membranes.

The history of the synthetic membrane in construction is no more than half a century old. We are now just at the beginning of a development that is certain to gain significance over the coming decades. The technical properties of these membranes are constantly being improved and the costs are on a competitive level with conventional façade constructions—in some cases actually cheaper. Because major structural and functional objectives can be achieved using extremely small amounts of material, it also represents an exceptionally sustainable option.

55 — For an outdoor festival, the architects developed a temporary bar as a soft, haptic and user-friendly object for an urban context. The bar is an inflatable pipe with a cavity worked into its surface that, when filled with water, becomes a cooling trough for drinks. The water's weight stabilizes and deforms the pneumatic object. The pipe is made of a natural rubber material that is highly elastic and weatherproof. Being elastic, the rubber reacts to the displacement of air and water and determines the shape of the object.
Trinkbrunnen, St.Pölten, 2003. Design: the next ENTERprise, Vienna.

Material follows Form

56 — The Serpentine Pavilion, temporarily installed in 2006, comprised three main structural elements: floor platform, circular translucent wall enclosure, and inflatable roof canopy. The circular enclosure is created by polycarbonate twin walls that are five meters in height with a space of 1.6 meters between the inner and the outer wall. The central space within the inner ring wall, which can accommodate up to 300 people, is activated in a number of ways depending on the time of day and the program. The Pavilion design incorporates a helium and air-filled inflatable roof that can be raised and lowered according to the activities within the structure. The balloon is loosely attached with ropes to steel supports and can be shifted four meters vertically, thus granting a view to the trees in the park from the inside. Opened and extended, the oval pneumatic structure reaches a maximum height of 24 meters. It was fabricated from semi-transparent PVC-coated polyester.
Serpentine Pavillon, London, 2006. Architecture: OMA, Rotterdam in collaboration with Arup, London.

Shaped – Inflated

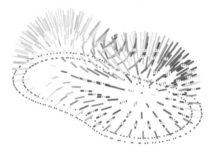

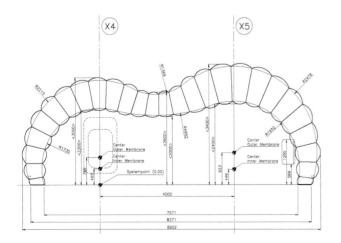

57 — Contemporary interpretation of ephemeral Japanese architecture in a modern material. The self-supporting pneumatic construction made of a double membrane and nicknamed "peanut" is stable from internal pressures of 1,000 pascals.

At internal pressures above 1,500 pascals, it can even withstand storms. The outer and inner shells are welded together to form an airtight seal, and are coupled at an additional 306 points with short cords that create a golfball pattern on both surfaces. The membrane is fabricated from Gore Tenara (PTFE textile with airtight coating) and is attached at the base to a box girder using heavy-duty zip fasteners. The entire construction is 9 meters long, 4.60 meters wide, 3.40 meters tall and weighs 150 kg. It takes just 10 minutes to let the air out of the structure and 2 hours to dismantle the entire pavilion.

Modern Teahouse. Design & planning: Kengo Kuma/form TL, Frankfurt/Main, 2007.

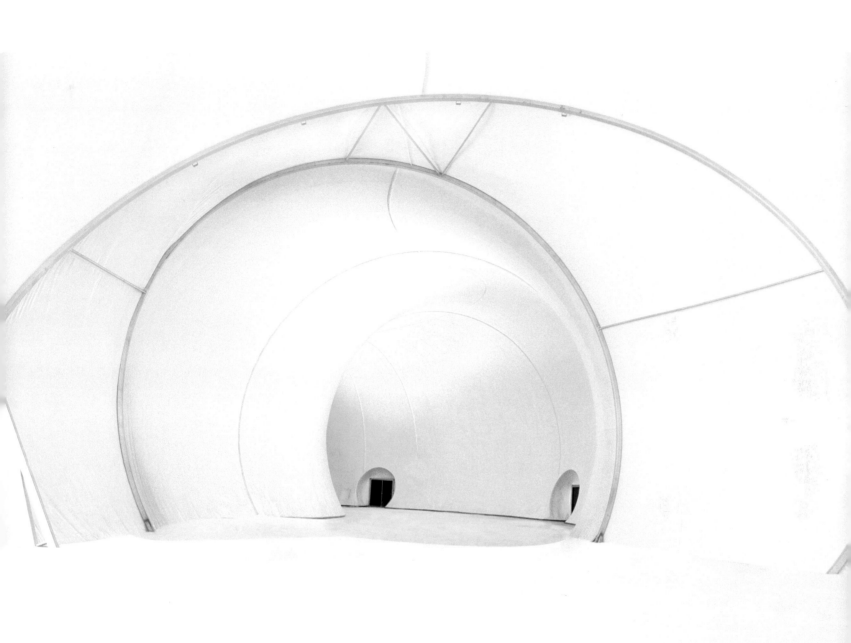

58 — The pressurized atmosphere inside the temporary pneumatic exhibition pavilion (covering an area of 1,240 m²) is numerically equivalent to the pressure experienced by placing one's head in 6 cm of water. The entire membrane weighs 3 metric tons and reaches up to 13.5 meters in height.
kiss the frog, temporary annex at the National Museum of Art, Oslo. Architecture: mmw architects of norway.

Shaped – Inflated

59 — 4,000 pneumatic ETFE cushions with diameters of up to 7.5 m make up the façade of the Water Cube swimming stadium with its total surface area of 100,000 m². The tessellated cells resemble a foam structure.
National Aquatics Center, Beijing, 2007. Architecture: China Construction. Design International (CCDI), Peddle Thorp Walker (PTW). Engineers: Arup, Beijing.

60 — Vacuum-supported bridge made of 40,000 plastic balls that are stabilized by an evacuated PVC foil. The span length of the structure is 10 meters.
Vacuum Bridge, 2006. Design & construction: TU Delft, Design of Construction Chair, Prof. Ulrich Knaack.

Inflated metal

Sheet metal can also be inflated. Pillow plates consist of metal sheets that are laser-welded at various spots and bulge out when filled with air pressure. This produces hollow spaces that can also be used to transfer fluids. The three-dimensional pillow plates are used in the food industry as heat exchangers for cooling or warming. They are manufactured with a pillow shape either on both sides or just one side and are easy to clean thanks to their smooth surface.[63]

Metal sheets placed on top of one another can be welded together along the edges, allowing them to be inflated as watertight "sheet metal pillows." In a development project at the ETH Zurich, Oskar Zieta from the Chair of CAAD (Prof. Ludger Hovestadt) has been looking at ways of using innovative industrial processes with the aim of manufacturing entire pieces of furniture or load-bearing structures from these pillows. **FIDU** technology allows thin metal sheets to be transformed into stable three-dimensional structures without requiring any forming equipment.
— **"Forming processes for sheet metal" page 112**

Deflated

A new field of research has recently turned its attention towards deflated structures—an absence of air can also be used for holding constructions in shape. **Vacuum**-supported structures contain a filling that is stabilized by the pressure of an evacuated shell. An everyday example is coffee powder that turns into solid blocks when sealed in vacuum packaging.

Researchers from the Design of Construction Chair at the TU Delft examined the combination of pneumatic objects filled with overpressure that are stabilized by an evacuated shell. Balls are sealed inside a plastic membrane and when the air is drawn out, the ball configuration compacts to the closest possible packaging of spheres. A prototype was built in the form of a stable vacuum bridge with 40,000 plastic balls held together by a vacuum pressure of -0.8 bar. The outer shell consisted of a PVC membrane with fabric reinforcement. With a width of 1.5 meters and a span length of 10 meters, the resulting bridge has dimensions that would even make it suitable for practical applications.[60]

61 — The inner space of the welded flat object that mutates into a stool is filled with liquid. The evolving forming process can be controlled via the liquid pressure and the sheet thickness. This method allows mass production with an individual touch, for each exemplar is unique due to the forming process.
FIDU, Free internal pressure forming. Design & development: Oskar Zieta, Zurich.

62 — Prototype of a bridge using the FIDU principle. Formed by water pressure, the sheet metal elements span a length of six meters and offer high material efficiency due to their low sheet thickness in comparison with conventional structures.
FIDU Bridge, 2007. Design & development: Oskar Zieta, Philipp Dohmen, Zurich.

The final shape is solely influenced by the contouring of the sheets, the form-critical welding spots on the surface, and the internal pressure used. The objects are "inflated" with water at pressures of between 6 and 50 bar, depending on the thickness and geometry of the material. Forms produced in this manner are more stable than equivalent forms made using similar amounts of folded metal sheets. At the same time, the process opens up a new formal language derived from the material's characteristics. Possible future applications could include transportable construction elements that are only inflated upon reaching the building site.[61, 64]

A prototype bridge made of **sheet steel** has already been developed using the FIDU process. Both the longitudinal supports that span 6 meters and the 30 transverse supports were laser-cut from sheet metal, then welded together, and finally inflated. Load test-

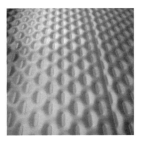

63 — Pillow plates made from laser-welded sheet metal.

ing of the structure demonstrates that the process would also be suitable for larger structural systems. Using thin-walled construction elements, the dead weight is around half that of structures that use standard steel profiles.[62]

The precursor to this technology is the internal high-pressure forming process that was developed for the automotive industry in which hollow forms are expanded by high internal pressure and pressed into a surrounding mold. But here, the size of the forms capable of being produced is still restricted by the maximum dimensions of the equipment.

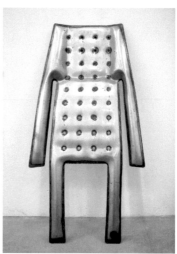

64 — The Chippensteel by architect Oskar Zieta is a stable hydroformed piece of furniture. It is made of two congruent metal sheets laser-welded together along the outer edges. Forming is controlled via additional spot welding on the surface. After "inflation", the four legs are bent down, folding the chair into its final shape. Stools and even lamps have been developed using the same principle of free internal pressure forming, FIDU.
Chippensteel, 2005. Design & development: Oskar Zieta, Zurich.

Shaped – Inflated

3.0 Digitized

Digital design has made a significant impact on new shapes in architecture. Even the most complex geometries are now calculable and thus buildable.

With digital planning and production tools, the language of graphic representation and its physical execution are drawing ever closer. A direct line of communication has evolved between design and its implementation. Design data can be exported straight from the computer into digitally-controlled equipment such as **CNC milling machines**, laser cutters, and **rapid prototyping** machines in order to fabricate specific components. CAD (Computer-aided Design) and **CAM** (Computer-aided Manufacturing) are merging into a single, integrated production process.

Forms are created by either adding material or taking it away. Milling machines and cutters remove material, while machines for rapid prototyping work by building material up and enabling forms to "grow."

66 — For a space without daylight, Gage/Clemenceau Architects designed a CNC-milled illuminated ceiling that consists of a cellular-shaped 3D structure. Milling gave an unusual and elegant surface quality to conventional plywood. The cellular modules were combined with translucent acrylic glass, producing a pleasant ambient lighting that makes the space appear more open and luminous, optically lengthening the room. Cellular Ceiling, New York, 2007. Architecture: Gage/Clemenceau, New York.

3.1 Cut & Carved

Materials can be digitally processed using laser cutters or laser milling machines. With the computerized numerical control (CNC) process, exact points in space can be defined and located. Cutting and milling machines are categorized by the number of spatial axes in which they can operate. The greater the number of axes, the higher the complexity of forms that can be produced.

If **plywood** is milled three-dimensionally, interesting structures and reliefs are created by the removal of layers. Milled wooden panels are available in a huge variety of milling patterns and surface treatments for decorative interior design. The panel size coincides with the standard formats of the base material.[65, 66, 71]

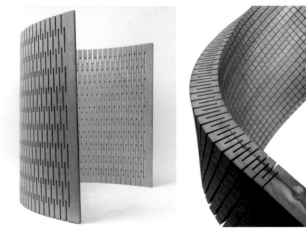

67 — Dukta: forming via CNC-milled longitudinal incisions or hand-milled longitudinal and lateral incisions. The longitudinal-only milling process is suitable for a wide variety of wood-based materials such as plywood and fiberboard panels. The more complex process of longitudinal and lateral milling is also suitable for solid wood. Development: Christian Kuhn and Serge Lunin, Zurich.

65 — 3D milled and lacquered wood surface.

Using linearly milled incisions, even stiff materials such as plastics or **metal** are made bendable and can be three-dimensionally formed. The many cutting patterns expand the range of possible deformations and applications. Initially rigid panels become as flexible as rubber mats.[67, 68]

68 — Continuously morphable metal surfaces can be fabricated by the XURF (eXpandable SURFaces) process. Like expanded metal, metal sheets are made ductile by incisions and then formed into 3D surfaces, with the extent of their ductility being determined by the distribution of the incisions. These incisions are calculated using a computer program and implemented using CNC laser or waterjet cutters. Development: Dr. Haresh Lalvani. Milgo/Bufkin, New York.

69 — A high degree of computer-aided production technology was required to make the 7,200 individual façade panels of the art museum. The surface design is based on pixellated landscape photos. A computer program transformed the images into an abstract pattern of indentations and protuberances. There are eight different depth levels of the perforations, as well as flat panels. The perforations and indentations overlap in different intensities. Around 1.5 million punctual deformations and as many round cut-outs cover the copper-sheet façade as semi-transparent ornaments. Due to the highly complex surface and the copper material, its appearance constantly changes, not only under different weather conditions and depending on the time of day, but also through patination over the years.
De Young Museum, San Francisco, 2005. Architecture: Herzog & de Meuron, Basel.

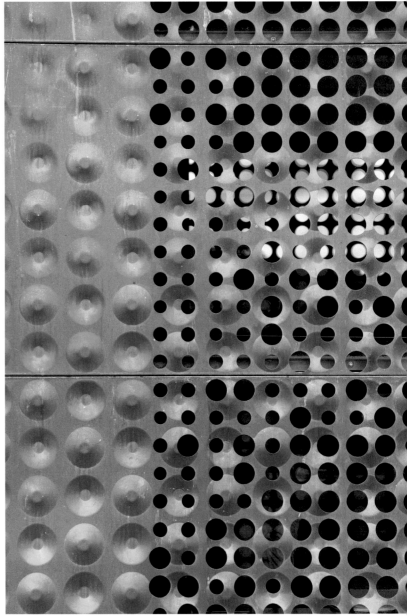

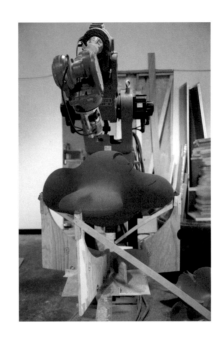

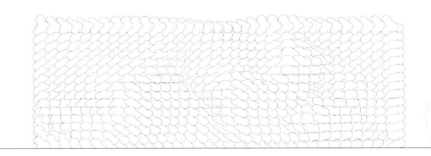

70 — "Blob Wall" is an innovative free-standing wall system that redefines architecture's most basic building unit, the brick. The "blob brick" is a tri-lobed hollow shape that is mass produced through rotational molding from a recyclable, lightweight and resistant plastic. The modular elements are then custom-shaped using the latest CNC technology. Each wall is assembled from individually robotically cut hollow bricks that interlock perfectly. This system can be used to create walls and spatial structures for indoor and outdoor applications.
BLOB WALL©. Design & development: Greg Lynn FORM, Los Angeles, in collaboration with Panelite and Machineous, Los Angeles.

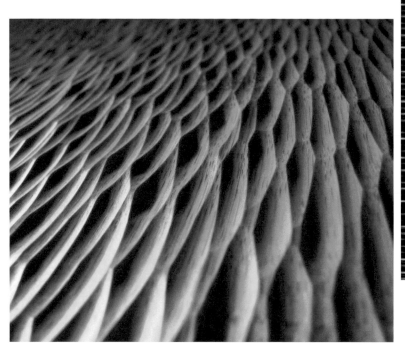

71 — Wooden panels can be turned into three-dimensional, haptic surfaces through five-axle milling technology. MDF and hardwood such as walnut, maple or oak are suitable as material. The surface can be treated in various ways using lacquer, stains, or oils.

3.2 Grown

CAD-generated geometries can be "printed out" three-dimensionally using a material additive process. The software divides the digital model into thin layers that are built up, one layer at a time. Different processes are available on the market, varying in terms of their fabrication method and surface quality. Smooth, high-quality surfaces can be produced using the **stereolithography process** in which liquid plastic (e.g. **epoxy or acrylic resin**) is solidified by a laser beam, one layer at a time.

For fabricating complex geometries, a suitable process is **selective laser sintering** whereby the object is solidified out of fused powder with successive new layers of material being added on top. Undercuttings are possible due to the gradual "growing" of forms in the z-axis. These shapes are impossible to fabricate in one piece with conventional technologies. Even functional hinges can be entirely "printed" in a single production step, emerging from the printer with completely finished moving parts.[78]

The materials used for selective laser sintering include **polyamide-based** plastics and mixtures based on metallic or mineral powder.

72 — Stereolithography process.

Due to the computerization of processes in rapid prototyping, the design and production stages are merging into one. The Sketch Furniture of the Swedish design group Front pushes this to extremes. Here, a sketch drawn in the air is directly materialized as a full-scale piece of furniture. The drawing movements are spatially scanned and processed into digital 3D files with the special program Motion Capture. This software was developed for digital animation in film and computer games. The recorded data are fed directly into a rapid prototyping machine and materialized layer by layer with liquid plastic using a stereolithography process. In just a few hours, the hand-drawn chair is finished.[79]

73 — Trabecula was inspired by the porous interior of bone. Polyamide-based 3D laser-sintered structure as a tray. Design: FOC, Janne Kyttänen.

74 — Möbius: laser-sintered textile that is sintered in one piece. It can be used to make clothing, handbags, or curtains. Design: FOC, Janne Kyttänen.

Because of the limited size of rapid prototyping machines, self-generating structures have so far been restricted to relatively small objects or pieces of furniture.

But the possibility of printing three-dimensional material using inkjet-style additive layering is a common process in prototype construction. Known as "**3D printing**," this principle has now been translated onto an architectural scale by the Italian engineer Enrico Dini.

Dini developed a room-sized 3D printer where the printhead—the real core of this innovation—consists of 300 individual inkjets and moves along a large framework construction. The entire machine can be assembled or dismantled by two people within the space of a few hours.

The architect Andrea Morgante (Shiro Studio) designed a free-form structure measuring 3 x 3 m that was created using this gigantic 3D printer.

The structure is self-supporting and requires no additional reinforcements. The material used is a stable mixture of inorganic binder with sand or mineral powder. It is added one layer at a time with no need for a negative mold or formwork. The artificial sandstone material with its marble-like structure exhibits good technical properties when subjected to tension, compression, and bending in material tests. Although this process is still a prototype at present, it represents a development that will certainly become significant for the construction industry in future.
— **"Rapid prototyping" page 113**

75 — Gyroid: polyamide-based laser-sintered table lamp. In natural science, gyroid refers to a triply periodic minimal surface that divides space in two directions to create congruent layers that do not intersect.
Design: materialise.mgx, Bathsheba Grossmann.

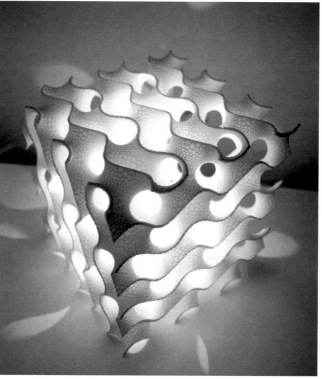

Digitized – Grown

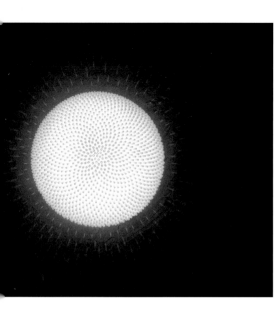

76 — 1597, indoor lamp made of laser-sintered poly-amide. The shape of this wall and ceiling lamp was inspired by the spiral arrangement of seeds in inflorescences.
Design: FOC, Janne Kyttänen.

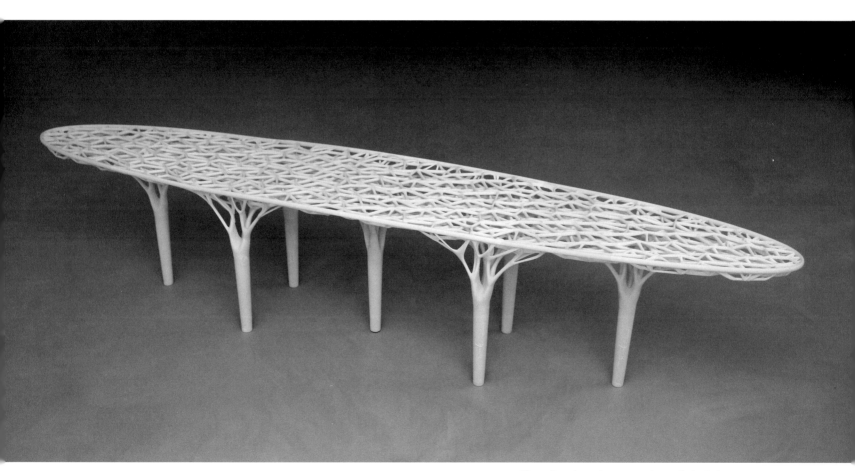

77 — The stable, three-dimensional shape of the Trabecula bench was inspired by bone structures. The unusually large, laser-sintered object is almost two meters long.
Design: FOC, Janne Kyttänen.

78 — Foldable stool with integrated
hinges "printed" three-dimensionally
from polyamide via selective laser
sintering. The stool emerges from the
laser-sintering machine in fully functional condition with no further assembly required.
One_Shot. Design: materialise.mgx,
Patrick Jouin.

Rapid prototyping
Sketch furniture
Swedish
2005
free hand sketch-
D digitalized

79— Freehand sketches are spatially
materialized using a special program.
The software records the movements in
digital form and relays the data to a
rapid prototyping machine that prints
out the objects in real size.
Sketch Furniture, Design: FRONT Design,
Sweden.

B — 3.2

Digitized – Grown

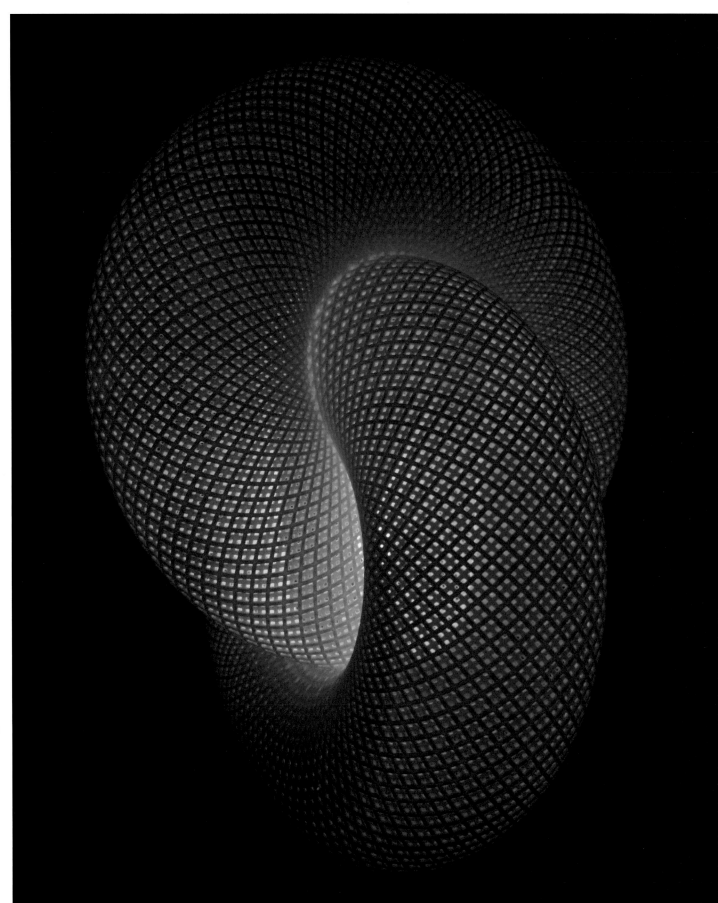

80 — Torus, laser-sintered floor lamp on polyamide-basis
Design: materialise.mgx,
Bathsheba Grossmann
& Jiri Evenhuis.

81 — Room-sized pavilion structure that was "printed" with a gigantic 3D printer. During the construction process, the printhead constantly distributes the structural ink onto the sand in layers between 5 and 60 mm thick. It takes around 24 hours for the material to solidify. The entire structure requires two weeks of printing by machine and one week of sanding by hand.
Radiolaria, 2009. Design: Andrea Morgante, Shiro Studio, London. Development: D-Shape, London.

Glossary

Solid surface materials

Material composition

Mineral powder or granulated stone and color pigments that are embedded in a synthetic resin matrix (acrylic or polyester-based).

Properties

The material is frost resistant, UV resistant, flame retardant, and has high impact resistance. It is non porous and therefore resistant to bacteria and mildew. Sheets with a thickness of 6 mm become translucent when backlit.

Product form

Available as sheets, molded pieces, or a two-component cast system. Sheet size (depending on manufacturer): up to approx. 95 x 370 cm. Thicknesses: 6 mm, 12 mm, 19 mm.

For the two-component cast system, fluid water-based acrylic resin is mixed with mineral powder. The material cures without shrinking, developing little heat.

Processing

Mechanical processing (similar to hardwood) via sanding, milling, and cutting. Two and three-dimensional thermoforming of sheet material is possible when heated to approx. 165°C.

Surface treatment

Printing via the "sublimation process" in which color pigments penetrate the surface matrix in a vacuum process. The material can then be repolished, thermoformed, or cut to size.

Beyond that, solid surface materials can also be stamped, milled, or sandblasted.

— page 51

Forming processes for sheet metal

Folding and bending

In the folding process, sheet metal is placed in a large press where it is forced into a V-shaped die by a punching tool, thereby permanently deforming the material. In order to bend sheet metal into curves, the material is fed through rollers of varying diameters.

Deep drawing

Deep drawing is generally carried out with a large press. The sheet material is held under tension in a blank holder to prevent the formation of wrinkles. A punch with the interior shape of the deep-drawn part is used to press the sheet into a preformed female mold.

Sheet hydroforming

In this type of deep drawing, a liquid medium is used to form the sheet metal.

Either the metal sheet is pressed into a solid die by a pressurized liquid medium, or a solid form punch is used to press the sheet against a pressurized liquid medium that replaces the die. As the punch is lowered, the rising pressure in the liquid medium forces the sheet into the exact shape of the punch.

This process can be used to achieve high surface quality because apart from the liquid medium, no mechanical tools touch the metal surface.

Internal high-pressure forming (IHU)

Process for manufacturing hollow metal objects in which steel tubes are expanded from the inside by a highly pressurized liquid medium and forced against an outer mold which forms them. It enables the fabrication of complex tubular geometries.

different types of rapid prototyping (handwritten note)

Free internal pressure forming (FIDU)

Two congruent metal sheets welded together at the edges are inflated from the inside by air or water pressure. The resulting pillow-shaped form is produced not by tools but by the geometry of the sheets. This technology only requires a fraction of the pressure needed in the IHU process.

Explosive forming

The controlled shockwave of an underwater explosion impacts on the material, which is pressed into a negative mold with great accuracy. The process is suitable for short production runs and prototypes with complex forms, as well as for large formats and high material thicknesses.
— **pages 84, 92**

Membrane materials for pneumatic constructions

Pneumatic constructions are made using either fluoropolymer (ETFE, THV) or PVC foils, or airtight-coated textiles based on glass-fiber, polyester, or fluoropolymer material.

Foils

ETFE (ethylene tetrafluoroethylene) is one of the most commonly-used membrane materials today. It is a synthetically-manufactured fluoropolymer based on fluorite—a widespread mineral. ETFE foils are highly UV-resistant and exhibit no yellowing or embrittlement, even after years of use. They are self-cleaning and flame-retardant, making them ideal for façade applications. Their transparency, light transmissivity, and material thickness can be varied according to requirements. They can be entirely recycled. The estimated lifespan of ETFE foil is around 25–30 years.

As foil, PVC (polyvinyl chloride) exhibits low stability and a high rate of thermal expansion. This makes it unsuitable for permanent outdoor applications but it can still be utilized for interiors. PVC is not easy to recycle and is not UV resistant.

Coated fabrics

MPTFE (polytetrafluoroethylene; brand names include Teflon) or silicon-coated glass fabrics are UV resistant and self-cleaning but susceptible to kinking due to the glass fiber content.

PVC-coated polyester fabric (PVC/PES) has good kink resistance and is thus suitable for repeated use in mobile or convertible structures.
— **page 85**

Rapid p[rototyping]

The automa... using a material ... generated file (ST... added as liquid or ...

Various typ... able, with the ma... generated.

Selective la[ser sintering]

Plastic pow[der] or sand admixture is locally bound (sintered) by a laser beam. The hardened powder supports the next layer above so that even highly complex and undercut forms can be produced without supports. The resulting surface has a grainy texture that can be finished by sanding.

Stereolithography

Liquid light-sensitive plastic is hardened one layer at a time by a laser beam. The object is built from the bottom upwards. Suitable for small production runs and prototypes with extremely high surface quality. Overhangs and cavities require the use of supports that need to be removed afterwards.

Three-dimensional printing

Like an inkjet printer that prints spatially, layers of powder with a binder are applied to build up three-dimensional objects. The process is relatively fast and inexpensive but the resulting surfaces are raw and coarse-grained. Starch, plaster, and plastic-based compounds can be used as materials. Colored material printing is also possible.

Fused deposition modeling (FDM)

A melted thermoplastic polymer mass is applied by a device that can move three-dimensionally, hardening upon impact. A low-cost but not particularly accurate process.
— **page 103**

C
114 – 153

Coats and Covers

1 — Refuge Wear–Habitent, 1992-93. Lucy Orta, Paris.

The housecoat

0.0 The housecoat

Ancient tent-like shelters needed to be light and transportable. The outer shell acted as an extended form of clothing that provided shielding against the elements. In traditional forms of housing, transparent sliding screens or curtains served as filtering layers that permitted air and daylight to enter but protected against direct sunlight and intrusive eyes.

Today, the façade continues to act as the functional clothing of a building in several ways, whereby the various layers perform different tasks. With our own clothing, we make ongoing modifications depending on the particular time of year or weather conditions. The outermost layer—the coat—changes with the seasons, while certain basics such as trousers and shirts are worn throughout the year. If we regard the building envelope as layering, we can deploy materials in architecture with similarly varying lifespans, replacing them as and when necessary. The outermost layer can be replaced at relatively short intervals to suit changing technical criteria or visual tastes. By contrast, the insulating layer is constrained by regular seasonal demands, while the water-conducting layer is a permanent requirement.

Functional layers such as insulation, waterproofing and solar protection are designed to filter out external influences at specific times and in specific amounts. Thus, daylight is allowed to enter for illumination purposes but excessive infrared radiation that would cause overheating is prevented. As complex materials such as translucent insulation, heat-storing glazing, and even self-darkening façade elements become available, new design possibilities are opening up. Building equipment that until now required external devices or components can increasingly be integrated within the surfaces or provided by ultra-thin coatings. Thus, functional hybrid materials are evolving that are highly efficient due to the minimized amount of material consumption in their production. With the integration of technology, the energy losses that occur when separate components are coupled together can be eliminated.

The façade of the future should be capable of responding to its environment like skin—its surface waterproof and yet permeable, reacting to external factors such as hot or cold temperatures, and capable of reporting damage and even healing itself. The necessary materials and technologies already exist.

2 — The building envelope as flexible "clothing" for the structure. Shigeru Ban's Curtain Wall House translates the Japanese tradition of light, translucent sliding walls into a contemporary architectural language. Curtains define the spatial perimeter in summer, while additional glass panels can be used in winter to close the façade. Curtain Wall House, Tokyo 1995. Architecture: Shigeru Ban Architects, Tokyo.

The housecoat

1.0 Protective

Our buildings are affected by weathering and mechanical wear. Time leaves its mark, causing materials to age. But the process is not always negative—sometimes an ageing effect is desired in order to lend surfaces a certain individuality. Particularly with natural materials such as wood, the patina is what brings the surface to life and imbues it with character. Some surfaces react to the elements by forming a protective layer that permanently shields the core material against weathering.

Such is the case with **Corten steel**. This alloy of copper, chrome, and nickel forms a consistent layer of iron oxide—otherwise known as rust—that behaves as a barrier and makes the material weatherproof. The intense rust-red surface also has a powerful aesthetic appeal.[11]

With the help of a special treatment, wood can also be equipped with additional properties to improve its resilience. **Thermally modified timber** (TMT) is produced by heating the material to around 200°C, thereby altering the wood cells and rendering them incapable of absorbing much water. Sugar-like components within the cellulose are caramelized during the process and help to preserve the wood. This treatment makes the material resistant to mildew, fungus, and moisture while turning it a darker and warmer color.[3]

If wood is exposed to even greater heat, the uppermost layer is charred and forms an effective natural barrier against insects and rotting. Despite producing a fascinating aesthetic, this traditional Japanese technique has largely fallen into obscurity. The process is carried out by hand and is quite time-consuming.[12]

3 — Thermally modified timber is moisture-proofed and gains a darker color via a heating process.

But the majority of modern material and design concepts do not favor surfaces that seem weathered or worn out. Glass, ceramics, and plastics are expected to retain their original pristine condition for years. And yet in contemporary urban environments, surfaces are exposed to increasing amounts of dust and dirt that infiltrate the pores and give the materials an unattractive appearance. Here, new coatings can help to keep surfaces permanently clean. The functional layers currently being developed are progressing into ever smaller realms. Some of them are no longer even visible to the naked eye.

1.1 Coatings

Self-cleaning layers

Surfaces that can repel dirt, break down pollutants, fight bacteria, and even "heal" themselves if cracks or scratches occur are now feasible thanks to pioneering technologies on a microscopic and nanoscopic scale.

Microstructuring is the key aspect of the much-cited **lotus effect**. Inspired by the natural structure of a lotus leaf, surfaces are designed with a nubbed texture that prevents water droplets from gaining a hold. Rain simply rolls off and takes the accumulated dirt with it. Paints for exterior façades imitate this microstructure. Their functionality remains undiminished for years, as long as no mechanical damage occurs.[4, 5]

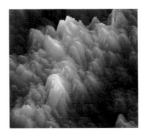

4 — Nanoscopic image of the surface structure of a lotus leaf.

5 — Lotus effect: Water droplets and dirt particles lie on top of the microscopic structure of a leaf surface that offers almost no potential for adhesion. The dirt particles picked up by the droplets of water are removed from the leaf surface.

Nanotechnology operates on an even smaller scale. One nanometer is equivalent to one millionth of a millimeter. The technology is based on the difference in physical properties between nanoscale particles and solid-state materials. Nanoscale particles are indiscernible because they are simply too small to interact with light in the visible spectrum. Their smallness is almost beyond imagination—the size of a football in comparison with the Earth is equivalent to the size of a nanoparticle in comparison with a football.

Given the environmental problems we are now facing, nanomaterials and nanocoatings have the potential to make a decisive contribution towards the energy efficiency of buildings. Maximum effects can be achieved using minimum amounts of material. Due to their high degree of specialization and the sparing use of materials in their production, nanomaterials can significantly reduce energy consumption. Furthermore, they can also help to lower maintenance costs. Self-cleaning nanosurfaces minimize the need for cleaning agents, while antibacterial surfaces reduce the need for disinfectants. In the long term, the environment is thus burdened with less chemicals.
— **"Nanomaterials" page 153**

6 — Water droplets running off hydrophobic façade coatings.

7 — Easy-to-clean enamel surface with droplet effect.

8 — A wall covering in the form of water-repellent "ceramic wallpaper" has been developed with a flexible substrate that is soaked with a ceramic-based dispersion. Although breathable and open-pored, the material repels water and oil, and can be used as a resistant surface in bathrooms.

Self-healing layers

High-quality stainless-steel or painted surfaces can be protected against mechanical wear by scratchproof nanolayers that form a glass-like silicon oxide coating.

Nanomaterials are manufactured based on substances such as carbon, silver, and ceramics. The decisive factor in determining nanoproperties is not the base material but the size of the molecular structure. Nanocoatings can equip their substrate materials with new characteristics that differ from their natural properties. This allows materials to be individually customized for specific purposes.

But it is now also possible for scratches and fissures to be "healed" from within the material itself. When materials are exposed to mechanical strain, even the finest of hairline fissures can grow over time into dimensions that might cause entire components to fail. The new development has thus a critically important role to play because it can offer real improvements in the safety of load-bearing structures or the inaccessible parts of high-rise buildings and bridge constructions. The durability of surfaces can be enhanced without extra maintenance, thereby helping to save raw materials.

Easy-to-clean surfaces can be produced with hydrophobic (water-repellent) or oleophobic (oil-repellent) coatings. In both cases, the attractive force of the material is reduced to such an extent that liquids contract into droplets and run off. Because the surfaces repel water and dirt, they are frequently used on ceramics, enamel, and glass in bathrooms. But textiles, metal, and wood can also be finished with hydrophobic coatings.[6–8]

10 — The principle of self-healing synthetic material is based on the circulation of repair fluid through a capillary system within the material.

Self-healing plastics imitate the function of natural skin. Skin is essentially a biological membrane that consists of layers of tissue interfused with fine blood vessels. In the event of injury, these vessels work together at closing the wound using healing components that are transported to the damaged area via the capillaries. This principle can be repeated as often as required at one and the same place.

9 — A photocatalytic glass coating causes the formation of a water film on the surface. This removes dirt when it runs off and keeps the glass clean.

Photocatalytic coatings remove organic pollutants in combination with water when exposed to UV radiation. **Titanium dioxide** is the catalyst in this process. The surface behaves in a hydrophilic (water-attracting) manner, causing water to form not into droplets but into an even film that "scours" impurities off the surface. Glass, ceramic, and concrete façade elements or even roof tiles can be treated with catalytic coatings. These surfaces require less frequent cleaning and inhibit the growth of moss or algae. A further benefit is the cost reduction in the case of inaccessible structures where professional cleaning services usually need to be employed. Photocatalysis also has an air purifying and antibacterial effect. The reaction breaks down chemical pollutants such as nitric oxides, ozone, and particulate matter.[9]

Sterile surfaces can be produced using silver nanoparticles. Applications include products such as antibacterial door handles, light switches, and flooring materials. This development is of particular interest to hospitals and clinics.

Emulating the network of blood vessels, researchers from the University of Illinois at Urbana-Champaign have developed a process based on the circulation of repair fluids within a material. This is done by fabricating a synthetic block of **epoxy resin** and integrating a framework of intersecting micro-channels that carry a special "healing liquid." If the surface is damaged or cracked, the liquid is moved via capillary action to wherever it is needed and reacts with the catalyst particles also embedded within the synthetic material, thereby filling any cracks or uneven areas. The process is repeatable because the substance is constantly redistributed throughout the entire system via the capillaries.[10]

The latest developments are not only restricted to synthetic surfaces. Researchers at the University of Stuttgart and the University of Duisburg/Essen have managed to integrate nanocapsules with an oily core into metal coatings. If the surface is mechanically damaged, the substance inside the nanocapsules is released and the damaged area is oiled to protect it against corrosion.

11 — Corten steel forms a weatherproof surface. In order to protect adjoining materials from rust staining, the reddish skin is coated with a transparent varnish.
Centro parroquial de Rivas-Vaciamadrid, 2008. Architecture: Vicens + Ramos Architects, Madrid.

12 — The Japanese architect Terunobu Fujimori has revived the traditional Japanese process of charring. Three planks are tied together and newspaper is packed between the planks. The newspaper is then set on fire. It takes around seven minutes for the required degree of charring to be achieved and the process is stopped by dousing the wood with water. The finished surface is not only extremely resistant, but also has great aesthetic appeal.
Charred Cedar House, 2007. Architecture: Terunobu Fujimori.

Adaptive layers

Adaptive and intelligent building envelopes that respond to external influences are no longer science-fiction. They can modify their transparency according to light conditions or mutate at the press of a button into view control or solar protection. The necessary technologies have already been developed.[17]

Switchable glazing is based on photochromic, electrochromic, thermochromic, or gasochromic processes that are differentiated by their triggering stimuli. Thus, glass panels can darken if voltage is applied, solar radiation is detected, the surface temperature rises above a certain point, or a particular gas is injected into the space between the panes.

Electrochromic glazing, for example, consists of two panels coated on the inner sides with tungsten oxide and laminated together with a conductive film. If voltage is applied, the glazing turns a blue color. If the electric current is discontinued, the glazing retains its existing color until voltage is reapplied. With this technology, mechanical screens such as blinds are no longer required.

The degree of light transmissivity is adjustable and the tinting can be individually modified to suit the particular lighting conditions. Visibility is maintained at all times and the building is protected against overheating in an energy efficient manner.[13]

Thermotropic shading systems switch between clear and light-diffusing states, depending on the ambient temperature. With intense sunlight and the corresponding increase in heat, the glazing turns opaque. But if the outside temperature drops back below a selected point, the panel becomes transparent. The laminated glass consists of a thin polymeric resin layer encased between two sheets of float glass. Nanocomponents in the resin are responsible for the switching effect. At low temperatures in winter, the warming sunlight is allowed to pass through unimpeded. But in summer, it is blocked by the opacity. No electricity sources or control systems are necessary to operate this system. The level of opacity and the switching temperature can be adjusted to suit individual requirements.[14]

13 — Switchable electrochromic glazing that uses color tinting to protect against overheating.

14 — Thermotropic glazing becomes opaque if the surrounding temperature rises above a certain point. This makes it possible to provide heat protection in summer without using any electricity.

Electrically switchable glazing that can change between transparent and translucent states is viable using **liquid crystal technology.**

15 — These changing rooms can be switched from opaque to transparent at the press of a button, offering a view of the interior if desired. Prada, NYC 2001. Architecture: OMA Rotterdam.

16 — Power-generating, self-darkening glazing. The surface acquires a color tint to protect against solar radiation while generating electricity via integrated photovoltaic technology.

The system here involves electro-optical laminated glass with a liquid crystal film embedded inside. By applying an electric current, the liquid crystals are transformed from their random light-diffusing state into an organized and transparent arrangement. This transparent state needs to be maintained with a constant supply of electricity. Mostly used as switchable view control glazing for interior applications, the material is also suitable for façades. In its opaque state, it provides an outstanding projection screen. The maximum dimensions are around 1 x 3 m.[15]

Scientists at the Eindhoven University of Technology in the Netherlands have recently developed a combination of electrically-switchable glazing and **photovoltaic technology.** Their power-generating façade panel is currently being developed for mainstream applications. It can be fabricated with different tinting colors and can switch between three defined settings—dark, translucent, and bright. The darker the setting, the more energy can be generated from the glazing.[16]

17 — The traditional façade is replaced by a multifunctional building envelope. Floor, walls, and ceiling merge into a single continuous shape and are fabricated from a plastic or glass material that is fitted with a <u>low-e coating</u> and <u>electrochromic film</u>. This minimizes thermal transmission and allows the surface to be switched from transparent to opaque or even to be entirely darkened as required. In addition, printed-on solar cells help to cover most of the building's electricity demand while only reducing light transmissivity by 20%. The relationship between the enclosed volume of the building and its surface area is optimized by the lenticular spheroid shape. Haus R1209, 2005. Development & design: Werner Sobek with Maren Sostmann, Werner Sobek Ingenieure, Stuttgart.

Protective – Coatings

1.2 Filters

Solar protection

Façades act as membranes that mediate between interior and exterior environments. Light, air, and moisture need to be exchanged in a controlled manner to ensure a comfortable indoor climate. The challenge here is to find the right balance at the right time. Daylight is desirable but should not be blinding. Fresh air is necessary but exhaust fumes and noise should be kept out. There are various elements that can serve as filter layers, helping to get the balance right. These are either permanently installed or can be controlled and adapted to meet changing requirements.

Solar and thermal protection coatings on double glazing have been a standard feature in the construction industry for decades. Thin layers based on metallic oxides block most of the radiant heat from the sun, while letting in the visible light. Neutral-colored **low-e (low emissivity) coatings** are suitable for thermal protection. In summer the coating reduces indoor solar gain and in winter it minimizes thermal loss. Low-e coatings can be applied to glazing and—in a recent development—even to foils, glass fabrics, and textiles.[20]

A new kind of textile has been developed with an adhesive coating on the back to provide a flexible and temporary form of view control and solar protection on glass panes. The silicon-based adhesive coating makes the fabric stick to almost any smooth, nonpo-

18 — Self-adhesive solar protection fabric with a silicon-based adhesive coating on its rear surface. Used for temporary privacy screens and antiglare protection, the material is simple to apply and can be subsequently removed without leaving any residue.

rous surface without the need for conventional glue. It can be removed without residue and can be used repeatedly without any deterioration in its adhesive force. This means that privacy and antiglare screens can now be installed with no need for fittings such as curtain rails—the material is attached directly to the pane.[18]

Light and shade on demand is also offered by adjustable pneumatic shading systems that are building envelope and solar protection element in one. They deploy a special type of **ETFE** "pillow" that consists of three layers of foil printed with different patterns. The patterns on the middle and outer layers complement one another. By changing the pressure of the inner chambers in the pillow, the layers can either be brought together or pushed a maximum distance apart. Thus, varying degrees of overlap regulate the intensity of incoming light.[19]

With façades, visual screening and solar protection can be integrated into insulating glazing with inserts made of textiles, metal mesh, **expanded metal**, wooden blinds, and light-diffusing plastic structures that redirect the rays of sunlight while ensuring visibility. The advantage of integration is that the filigree materials do not get dirty or dusty. Fine structures such as textiles for view control can also be directly laminated into multilayer acrylic glass.[21–23]

19 — Patterns of overlapping dots are printed onto the middle and outermost layers of a three-ply pneumatic ETFE pillow as contrasting and complementary graphics. Using a system of valves, the air pressure inside the pillow chambers can be controlled so that the layers either press up against each other or are spaced apart. In the first case, the patterns on the two foils complement one another and the transparency of the pillow is reduced to 20%. In the second case, the patterns open up and allow more daylight to enter the interior.
Art Center College of Design, Pasadena, USA, 2004. Architecture: Daly Genick Architects. Graphic design of pillows: Bruce Mau Design.

20 — The façade consists of crystalline-arranged elements that act as an optical filter. The individual glass
panes are treated with a low-e thermal protection
coating and a reflective solar protection coating. The
immediate surroundings are mirrored on this projection
screen as an abstract pixelated image. Due to the
varied geometric orientation of the different surfaces,
a camouflage effect is produced that seems to demate-
rialize the façade. Viewed from the interior, large areas
of transparent glazing alternate with individual sections of opaque glass.
Trutec Building, Seoul, 2006. Architecture: Barkow
Leibinger Architects, Berlin.

21 — Laminated into multilayer glazing, this fabric with a copper coating on one side changes transparency depending on the solar angle of incidence. The reverse side of the fabric is black, while the metallic copper front can also be individually designed using digital printing.

22 — Double glazing with embedded expanded metal that provides angle-selective solar protection. The result is antiglare lighting in the room interior, while the tightly meshed material also provides effective privacy from the outside world.

23 — Prism panels made of highly transparent acrylic glass reflect the direct sunlight but allow diffused light to enter the room. Customized arrangements of the prism structure enable the light management to be optimized, allowing the prisms to deliver large quantities of light deep into the interior space.

Panels or fabrics attached to the exterior side of a façade provide effective solar protection because thermal radiation is captured before it can enter the building. Furthermore, movable and external elements can be flexibly adjusted to individual situations. Materials taken from the industrial context such as **metal fabric** and expanded metal are particularly suitable here due to their stability and aesthetics. For example, non-rip and flexible metal fabrics are normally used for conveyor belts. But in the architectural context, they are deployed because of their fascinating visual quality and because they reflect the incoming sunlight according to their multidirectional metal surface.[24]

A façade that can dynamically adapt to various conditions has been developed as a research prototype. The surface is made up of "pixels," each containing four triangular tiles that are moved by wires of **shape memory alloy** (SMA) and that enable incoming and outgoing light to be controlled. Each pixel has 255 different states between fully open and fully closed, and a microcontroller regulates the electricity current that is supplied to the pixels 20 times a second. The façade can be used to generate low-resolution images, patterns, and even simple animations. The project has thus found an intelligent solution to the conflicting demands of providing façade functions such as view, natural light, and ventilation for the interior, while at the same time presenting a display surface for advertising where openings are considered an irritation. In this example, the openings themselves become the graphically animated surface.[25]

24 — The façade of the apartment block has a multilayer structure. Using adjustable elements, residents can regulate the view, amount of shade, and degree of privacy by moving the internal wall panels and external metal curtains. This stainless-steel wire mesh originates from the field of conveying equipment and is commonly used for conveyor belts in industrial bakeries. The curtains are motorized and can be individually controlled by the residents. Hohenbühlstrasse apartment block, Zurich, 2004. Architecture: agps Architecture, Zurich.

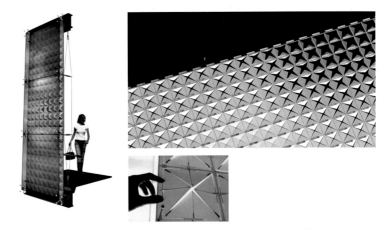

25 — This electrographic surface makes it possible to build a dynamic façade that can be used to control the natural lighting while simultaneously generating low-resolution images or videos on its exterior side. The "pixels" are actuated by integrated microcontrollers via shape memory alloy (SMA) wire. Pixel Skin, 2002. Design: Orangevoid, London.

Pollution filters

Natural phenomena such as sunlight are not all that the building envelope needs to filter out. We are increasingly exposed to environmental pollution that can impair the quality of our lives. Especially in dense urban settings, we are constantly surrounded by dirt, noise, and various types of radiation. Particulate matter generated by industrial, domestic, and vehicular combustion is a problem that markedly reduces the air quality in our cities. Building surfaces can act here as filters to protect indoor and outdoor living spaces.

Plants have the characteristic of absorbing CO_2—the compound partially responsible for the greenhouse effect. The idea of integrating green areas within architectural concepts is not new. Even in the ancient world, buildings were often covered with a layer of vegetation such as vines to protect them from the sun and provide a buffer against the summer heat. Furthermore, green areas on roofs or façades have an air-purifying effect that helps to improve the microclimate. The plants and their substrates absorb and filter

26 — Olivine: a green mineral that absorbs CO_2 and can be used as an additive in concrete.

27 — An air-purifying modular system with a titanium-dioxide-based photocatalytic coating. The modules can be added together to cover surfaces of customizable size within the urban environment. They can also be utilized in interior settings as wall coverings, suspended ceilings, or freestanding elements. proSolve370e. Design & development: Elegant Embellishments, Berlin.

particulate matter that is harmful to humans. But while green roofs have now become technically advanced, green walls have only been implemented with increasing frequency in recent years. They help to dampen noise and make for visually appealing surfaces within the urban environment. Most of these systems employ a "curtain" of plants designed to prevent damage to the building by roots or moisture. Heavy soil is replaced here by substrate materials such as felts or foams that are kept moist with nutrient-enriched water via an irrigation system.[30]

Concrete that absorbs CO_2 can be produced by adding **olivine**. This greenish silicate material—also used in the fabrication of heat-resistant glazing—can replace sand and gravel in the concrete mix. Studies conducted by cement manufacturers show that olivine concrete can store 10 times more CO_2 than the amount set free during its production.[26]

Mineral plasters and façade paints can be furnished with air-purifying, **photocatalytic technology.** Façades, walls, and road surfaces can thus make an active contribution to the quality of urban life by filtering

28 — Electrostatically charged surfaces attract small particles. R&Sie Architects translated this phenomenon into a study for a filtering façade in their design for a building in heavily polluted Bangkok. An electrostatically charged skin of aluminum mesh is used to attract particulate matter from the surroundings. This is then deposited on the building as an iridescent gray layer that becomes a protective membrane between the controlled environment of the interior and the pulsating chaos of the surroundings. The dust gives shape to the monolithic building, while simultaneously purifying its immediate environment.
Dusty relief, Museum for Contemporary Art, Bangkok, 2002, Architektur: R&Sie(n).

29 — High-tech curtain with interwoven ultrafine metallic threads that shield shortwave electromagnetic radiation and can also be utilized to prevent data theft from WLANs.

the air. Photocatalytically enhanced cement can be processed into road surfacing or paving stones made of concrete that are capable of breaking down pollutants. Depending on the UV intensity which triggers the reaction, photocatalytic surfaces can remove between 40% and 90% of the nitric oxides and other pollutants from the air.

For indoor climate regulation too, products such as paint, curtains, and carpets have now been developed that autonomously purify the air and transform pollutants such as nicotine and formaldehyde into water vapor and CO_2. Because the pollutants are actually converted and not simply absorbed, the effect of the material does not diminish over time.

Not only are we surrounded by discernable sensory impressions such as smells, but there are also various types of radiation present in our environment. A curtain material with ultrafine metal threads woven into the fabric has been developed that can shield up to 90% of electromagnetic waves. Cell-phone radiation and electrosmog can thus be kept away from certain spaces. The exceptionally thin metallic mesh integrated within the fabric reflects most of the incoming radiation. But the **electromagnetic protective curtain** also works in the other direction—it can be used to "fence in" wireless local area networks (WLANs). Data can then only be exchanged with the landline network via a registered WLAN station located inside the same room. This prevents external users from logging onto unencrypted networks. Despite the metal threads, the curtain can be easily washed and has a flowing, textile feel.[29]

30 — Surfaces planted with boxwood trees adorn the façade of this fashion store in Seoul. The vertical garden consists of substrate-filled steel boxes that are connected to an irrigation system. On the ground floor, air-purifying mats of moss are attached to the walls. The plants take root in a geotextile and require no soil. Watered by a specially installed mist system, the green walls improve the ambient air and filter out pollutants.
Ann Demeulemeester Shop, Seoul, 2007. Architecture: Mass Studies, Seoul.

2.0 Insulating

2.1 Climatic insulation

For people to feel comfortable inside a building, certain basic climatic requirements need to be fulfilled. Temperature, humidity, and air circulation are critical parameters. Insulating layers buffer temperatures between the interior and exterior.

In recent years, there has been a major increase in the demands placed upon the performance of thermal protection. But to save walls from adding increasingly thick layers of insulating material, there is now an urgent need for efficient materials that can deliver enhanced insulating properties at the same thickness.

Fibrous and air-entraining materials—such as felts made of animal hair or plant fiber, and panels made of mineral fiber or wood wool—make highly suitable insulating materials. Porous materials are another good option. Commonly used materials are expanded polystyrene, rigid polyurethane foam, expanded glass, and expanded clay. The smaller and more numerous the pores, the better the insulating performance of the material, because the air or gas in the pores hinders the transfer of heat. The property at hand is the thermal conductivity of a building material.

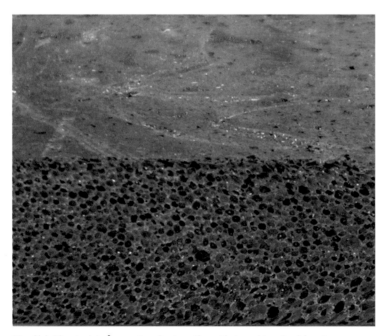

31 — Hybrid material of cement and polyurethane that combines load-bearing, fireproof, and insulating properties.

New insulating materials

Although foamed insulating materials have been used in construction for a long time, new improvements continue to be made.

New mixtures combine different characteristics and can produce materials with exceptional functionality. One pioneering composite of **polyurethane** and **cement** is lightweight, insulating, and load-bearing at the same time. This hybrid material was developed at the Institute of Composite and Biomedical Materials at the University of Naples. It combines the thermal and acoustic insulating properties of the organic polymer with the excellent mechanical

32 — Polystyrene spheres with added graphite exhibit up to 20% greater insulating capacity due to their reflective properties in the infrared spectrum.

qualities of hydraulic cement—including thermal stability, fire resistance, and vapor permeability. Rather than simply adding one material to the other, the components here are bonded together at such an integral level that they form an entirely new and unique hybrid material with the combined properties of the two ingredients. The result is a new material which is both structurally stable and insulating at the same time.[31]

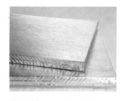

33 — Vacuum insulation panels.

The insulating properties of **expanded polystyrene panels** (EPS insulation) can be improved by up to 20% by mixing graphite powder into the material matrix. The base material of polystyrene granules is expanded with the help of steam and then modified with graphite. The grayish colored material can either reflect or absorb heat radiation in the infrared spectrum, thereby significantly improving thermal insulation. This makes it possible to save resources because the required insulating performance can now be attained using less material than with conventional EPS.[32]

Efforts to minimize the thermal conductivity of air or gases enclosed in porous structures have led to further innovative approaches to building materials—vacuum and nanopore insulation.

Neither of these technologies is actually new. Vacuum insulation panels have been used to insulate refrigerators for decades, while nanofoam was developed as early as 1930 and has been utilized by NASA as insulation material for aerospace applications since the 1950s.

So the transfer of these technologies to the conservative field of the building industry comes with a delay of decades.

Translucent insulation

Translucent insulation is based on light-transmissive capillary structures made of glass or plastic that enable solar energy to be used as a passive heat source on exterior walls. This type of façade insulation minimizes heat loss through the outside walls while simultaneously harnessing the incoming thermal energy.

34 — The lightest solid matter in the world—aerogel—was discovered in 1930 by the chemist Samuel S. Kistler. The material consists of 99.8% air that is enclosed in tiny nanopores, making it an ideal insulating material. NASA uses the silica foam as insulation in spacesuits and spacecraft. Aerogel has only recently appeared on the market as a high-tech insulating material for architectural purposes.

Vacuum insulation is fabricated in panels consisting of an open-celled high-strength core (e.g. pyrogenic silica or polyurethane foam) and an outer gas-tight membrane of aluminum foil or aluminized plastic film. The open-celled foam structure allows the element to be evacuated while retaining its inherent stability. The thermal conductivity of the overall composite ranges from 0.004 to 0.008 W/mK in comparison with EPS that ranges from 0.035 to 0.045 W/mK. However, this exceptional property can only be maintained if the outer membrane of the vacuum-insulated panel (VIP) remains undamaged. For this reason, the panels have to be manufactured in the required dimensions with no possibility for cutting them into shape at a later stage.[33]

Tiny **nanopores** measuring just five millionths of a millimeter in diameter are the basis of **aerogel**. It has the lowest-known density of any solid matter and consists of 99.8% air with the rest being a silica nanofoam. Also called "solid smoke" on account of its appearance, aerogel usually comes in blocks and is extremely light and strong—it can support up to 4,000 times its own weight but breaks easily if pressure is not evenly applied. Its pores offer excellent thermal insulation as they are smaller in diameter than both the wavelength of solar radiation and the mean free path of air. To make it easier to handle, aerogel is processed into granules that can be used in the construction industry as a filling for façade panels. This creates translucent building elements that offer exceptional thermal and acoustic insulation, while also being UV resistant and fireproof.[34]

35 — Insulated glass panels with translucent insulation. Filigree glass tubules measuring 10 mm in diameter and with a wall thickness of just 0.1 mm are layered inside the glass panels. Gluing is not possible due to the impairment of the optical effect.
The 80 mm long tubules ensure privacy and improve the direct heat gain and daylight yield of north-facing rooms, while also providing sound insulation.
Netherlands Embassy, Berlin, 2003. Architecture: OMA Rotterdam.

Solar radiation that is captured by the capillaries is stored by the solid and mostly black-coated heat-absorbing wall. The wall then serves as time-delayed solar heating for the interior space behind it.

The capillary materials are normally placed between panes of insulating glazing or covered with translucent glass plaster and glass fleece to prevent them from collecting dust.

In winter, when the sun is at a low angle, incoming light is directed to the absorption surface due to the horizontal alignment of the capillaries. In summer, reflectance on the glass plaster or in the capillaries prevents the sunlight from reaching the building wall and thus no extra heat gain is generated.

But translucent insulation panels can also be deployed as light-diffusing façade elements. The material ensures outstanding levels of daylight capture, distributing the light deep into the interior and at the same time providing sound absorption.

Insulating glass elements with inlaid PMMA capillaries or glass tubules can be used for this purpose.[35-37] **Aerogel granules** with their nanofoam structure can also serve as translucent insulation, providing the fill material in glass panels.

36 — Translucent insulation made of light-diffusing PMMA synthetic capillaries.

Coats and Covers

37 — Buildings seemingly made of light represent an addition to the existing museum complex. The double-layer glass assembly offers excellent solar and antiglare protection. The exterior layer consists of double inter-locked glass planks with a sandblasted finish that contains light-diffusing <u>translucent insulation</u> in between. The inner layer is laminated low-iron glass with an acid-etched finish. The diffused light ensures that the exhibition spaces are evenly illuminated during the day, while at night the structures appear to glow thanks to the filtering of the interior light.
Nelson-Atkins Museum of Art, Kansas City, 2007. Architecture: Steven Holl Architects.

Insulating – Climatic insulation

Latent heat storage

Walls with integrated latent heat storage materials can help to level out climatic peaks in buildings. The key to this technology is **phase change materials** (PCMs) that are manufactured on the basis of paraffin or salt hydrate. Upon reaching a predetermined critical temperature (e.g. 22°C), their physical state begins to change from solid to liquid. During this phase change, thermal energy is drawn from the surroundings and stored in the PCM. The room temperature is thus prevented from rising any further and the climate is passively controlled.

If the ambient temperature then drops below the critical point—such as in the evening—the process is reversed. The liquid PCM crystallizes back into a solid state. The absorbed energy is released, warming the room. Meanwhile the PCM regenerates itself for the next phase of energy absorption. Thus, the room is heated and cooled without any external energy input.

Microencapsulated PCMs based on **paraffin** can be integrated in gypsum plaster or gypsum plasterboard. If used for interior construction, these materials can reduce the overall heat load of a building. The heat storage capacity of 2 cm of plaster containing 30% PCM is equivalent to an 18 cm thick concrete wall or a 23 cm thick brick wall. This opens up whole new perspectives for lightweight construction, making complex and expensive air conditioning technology a thing of the past.[38]

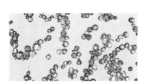

38 — Microcapsule structures in phase change material (PCM) that regulate the room climate by changing between liquid and solid states.

39 — Latent heat storage material in the form of salt hydrate incorporated within polycarbonate panels.

Special glazing with integrated PCMs can provide translucent insulation, overheating protection, and thermal storage at the same time. Here, latent heat storage is provided by **salt hydrate** that is hermetically sealed inside polycarbonate containers. A layer of prismatic glass encased in the outermost airspace of the glazing system prevents overheating in summer by reflecting steep-angled incoming solar radiation.

By contrast, the relatively shallow-angled sunlight in winter is allowed to penetrate and strike the PCM module that stores the incoming energy by melting. If room temperature drops below 26°C, the salt hydrate crystallizes and releases the energy back into the room as pleasant radiant heat. So rather than the common perception of the glass façade as being cool, it is transformed into an additional heating surface that improves thermal comfort. PCM insulated

40 — Triple glazing system with prismatic glass and salt hydrate latent heat storage in the airspace. The glazing reflects the light from the high-standing summer sun, while allowing the light from the low-standing winter sun to enter. The system is both translucent insulation and heat storage in one.

glazing units are currently available in dimensions of 280 x 150 cm with a thickness of 79 mm.[39-42]

PCMs for enhancing the interior climate of existing buildings are also available, again based on salt crystals. Modern office buildings with large amounts of glazing often suffer from overheating in summer. But instead of upgrading with an air conditioning system, the building can be retrofitted with PCM elements. The material is sealed inside aluminum pouches that are simply laid onto suspended ceilings. The average lifespan of PCM is more than 25 years without any loss of efficiency—far longer than conventional air-conditioning equipment. In extensive field tests, room temperatures could be lowered by as much as 6°C.[43]

41 — Insulated glazing façade elements with embedded latent heat storage.
Apartments for senior citizens in Domat, 2004. Architecture: Schwarz Architektur, Zurich.

42 — PCM façade elements blend smoothly into the design concept and enhance both the climatic properties and the daylight yield.
Marché International Support Office, Kemptal, 2007. Architecture: Beat Kämpfen, Büro für Architektur, Zurich.

43 — Phase change material sealed in pouches that can be used for retrofitting existing buildings to improve the indoor climate.

44 — Sound-absorbing covering of pyramid panels made of melamine resin foam coated with a polyurethane skin.
Casa da Musica, Porto, 2005. Architecture: OMA, Rotterdam.

2.2 Acoustic insulation

In the construction context, a distinction is made between air-borne and structure-borne sound insulation. Structure-borne sound insulation absorbs the transmission of impact sound within a building component—underneath screed, for example. The materials utilized here are elastic and need to be capable of absorbing the applied impact energy. Rubber and cork granulate mats are suitable, for example.

Materials that absorb airborne sound "swallow" noise from acoustic sources within a space. Particularly significant here is sound absorption in which the sound waves are dissipated by converting them into thermal energy via friction. Fibrous, porous materials such as fabrics are suitable. Carpets, cushioning, and heavy curtains are thus highly effective in improving the acoustics of reverberant spaces. Panels of compressed **aluminum fiber** are also

45 — Sound-absorbent panels made of compressed aluminum fiber, designed for use as wall and ceiling coverings including for outdoor locations and damp interiors.

suitable for **sound absorption.** Due to their rustproof properties, they can also be deployed outdoors or in damp interiors such as indoor swimming pools. They are non-flammable and can easily be bent due to their structural characteristics.[45]

Porous **foams** can also be utilized to absorb sound. **Melamine resin foam** with its fine and open-celled structure offers exceptional insulation charac-

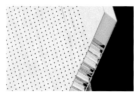

46 — Acoustic partitions with a foam core covered with a woolen felt fabric
47 — Sound-absorbing honeycomb panels with room-sided perforation.

48 — Microperforated honeycomb panels.

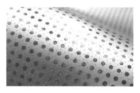

49 — Microperforated foil.

teristics in the medium and high-frequency ranges. The foam is also flame-retardant and again suitable for damp interiors and indoor swimming pools. Combined with sound-permeable fabric, it can be made into visually appealing partitions that can be deployed to improve the acoustics in residential or office environments.[46]

Acoustic elements made of melamine resin foam can be spray-coated to suit individual color preferences. The fine pores of the foam are not blocked by the paint and the material's excellent sound-absorbent and fire-resistant qualities are preserved. The foam can also be coated with a sonically transparent polyurethane skin that makes the surface easier to clean.[44]

A surface with perforations and a hollow space behind it will also act as a **sound absorber. Honeycomb panels** are a good option here—their cores with innumerable tiny cavities have a sound-absorbing effect. The surfaces of these lightweight acoustic panels can be designed to suit individual requirements. One alternative is to cover them with a real wood veneer.[47]

If the perforations are extremely small—between 0.2 mm and 0.8 mm in diameter—the material is referred to as **microperforated.** Suitable base materials are transparent, translucent, or printed polycarbonate foils, acrylic sheets, or honeycomb panels with microperforated surfaces that reduce the reverberation period in the medium and high-frequency ranges. It is important here to ensure sufficient distance between the microperforated material and the sound-reflecting surface behind it.

Translucent elements can be blended almost invisibly into the architectural concept. Microperforated foils can also be installed beneath thermoactive ceilings as they do not impede the heating or cooling effect. Because they are resistant to moisture, they can also be deployed in damp interiors. If the materials are printed, they can be utilized in UV-stable versions that can also provide solar protection if installed beneath glass roofs.[49]

3.0 Visual

A desire for visually opulent surfaces has returned, demonstrated by the showcasing of surfaces with ornaments, color, or light. In contemporary design, a new sensualism has replaced the modernist austerity whose strict aesthetics dominated a large proportion of 20th-century architecture. The design of surfaces has always carried high significance, codifying buildings or spaces within specific cultural or social hierarchies. This is particularly true of prestigious buildings and residences where wall paintings or façade ornaments are intended to convey messages that emphasize the status of the building and its owner. Today, ornaments are no longer manifestations of power, but they do underline a building's identity and can emphasize its function.

50 — Diaphanous honeycomb panel with pixel effect.

Even complex forms can now be digitally designed. The results can be sent directly to computerized manufacturing technology such as CNC machines and digital printers. Images and reliefs can be cut from virtually any type of material. Because these technologies are so easy to handle, bespoke surfaces can be individually designed and cut to shape for each new project.

51 — Translucent concrete slats with a cross section of 6 x 12 cm as diaphanous shading elements. The material is based on a special additive in the concrete mix that allows light to pass through the concrete. The end product is extremely stable and weighs 30% less than traditional concrete. Furthermore, it does not absorb water.
ICA office building, Mexico City, 2009. Architecture: Prof. Peter Ebner, Prof. Javier Sanchez, Munich/Mexico.

52 — Privacy screen with directional visibility film that only appears transparent from a certain angle.
ZKU64 Dental Clinic, Berlin, 2005. Architecture: Graft Architects, Berlin.

3.1 Diaphanous

Translucent surfaces exert a particular fascination because they blur the objects, spaces, and movements behind them into abstract patterns of light and shadow. Diaphanous materials and perforated surfaces are suitable for achieving this effect.[50]

Even solid **concrete** walls can become **translucent** with an innovative material mix. Mexican engineers have developed a recipe that is light transmissive. What is more, the material is extremely strong despite being one third lighter than traditional concrete. The manufacturing process is no different than normal concrete except that special cement and additives are used to give the material its diaphanous property.[51]

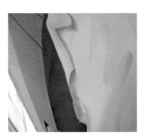

53 — Dichroic film with color-changing effects produced by the refraction of light within the film that can include up to 200 layers. Light and color produce abstract surface patterns that change with the viewer's perspective.

One type of surface that changes between translucent and transparent states depending on the viewing angle is based on a **microstructured film**. The material was originally developed for security purposes—restricting the viewing angle on computer screens so that only the person immediately in front of the monitor has clear visibility. For anyone else passing by, the screen appears blurred and details are indecipherable. When attached to glass façades or interior walls, the material exhibits an intriguing visual quality because it keeps changing with the viewer's movements.[52]

54 — Translucent backlit solid surface material for kitchen installation. Milan 2007. Design: Jean Nouvel.

55 — Natural stone calibrated to thicknesses between 0.3 and 1.0 mm is laminated onto glass with a PVB film. Due to its low thickness, the stone material is translucent and can be backlit.
The composite panels measure around 2.80 x 1.40 meters.

56 — Inlay material: grasses laminated between two polymer panels.

Some materials become **translucent** at a certain thinness when backlit. Even **natural stone** can now be sliced into millimeter-thin panels that enable a backlighting effect. In this instance, the material has to be further stabilized by laminating it onto glass. The resulting composite can then be utilized as a standard building component.[55]

The group of **inlay materials** represents a modern interpretation of the traditional craft of marquetry. Various objects such as plant fibers, petals, mother-of-pearl tesserae, or wood veneers are laminated between two transparent plastic or glass panels to produce a semitransparent material. This durable lamination gives the inlaid object a luminous brilliance while protecting it against both weathering and UV radiation.[56]

Semitransparent or perforated materials installed as façade layers create a sense of depth that lends the space or building a vibrant and often oscillating quality.

This effect can be produced by metal mesh structures that reflect the light in a special way. Layered perforated metal sheets or printed patterns will produce a **moiré effect** that renders a flickering impression of movement on the surface.[57, 60]

Honeycomb or tubular structures draw the viewer's attention in a special manner. Viewed from the front, the material has an open structure that makes it see-through. But as the viewing angle becomes more acute, visibility is blocked by the walls of the cell structure and the material appears nontransparent. The transparency of the material thus changes with the particular viewpoint.[58]

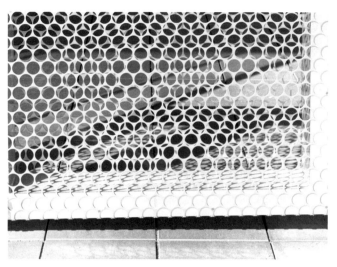

57 — Gate structure made of 2 mm thick perforated <u>stainless-steel sheets</u> with varying hole size. The gap of 15 cm between the two layers produces a moiré effect. Gatehouse, Ditzingen, 2007. Architecture: Barkow Leibinger Architects, Berlin.

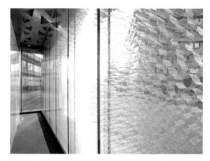

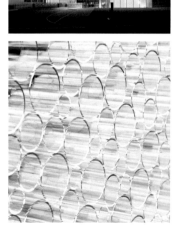

58 — View control was provided for a company gatehouse by cutting sections of standard <u>acrylic glass pipes</u> with diameters ranging between 4 and 14 cm to a length of 10 cm to match the depth of the façade. The pipes were then invisibly glued together. Panels of pipes measuring approx. 1.35 x 4.25 meters were processed into prefabricated façade elements. The structure ensures privacy for the security officers without impairing their view. Gatehouse, Ditzingen, 2007. Architecture: Barkow Leibinger Architects, Berlin.

Visual – Diaphanous

59 — Industrial <u>expanded aluminum</u> with a thickness of 3 mm was used to clad the New Museum in New York. The material is mounted several centimeters away from the underlying layer. Animated by the changing daylight, the multifarious angles of the mesh surfaces produce reflections that make the building appear light and almost unrealistically ephemeral. The individual metal components are joined together with an overlap of 25 mm so that the resulting shell appears to wrap the entire building in a seamless skin.
New Museum, New York, 2007. Architecture: SANAA, Tokyo.

Visual – Diaphanous

60 — The façade consists of one perforated and one printed <u>aluminium panel</u>. Both layers exhibit the corporate "cannage" pattern. Installed between the two layers is an illumination system that further intensifies the façade's moirē effect at night. When viewed from afar, the building has an immaterial and almost ghostly quality thanks to the shimmering luster of its skin.
Dior Ginza, Tokyo, 2004. Façade design: Office of Kumiko Inui, Tokyo.

Visual – Diaphanous

3.2 Imaging

Individually designed patterns, ornaments, and images can be applied to surfaces using modern **CNC milling technology.** Large-scale images can be milled using the linear computer-based Vectogramm process. First, the image is converted into 256 shades of gray. These gray values are then used to generate a machining file that controls the CNC milling machine. At close range, the finished surface exhibits an abstract texture. But when viewed from a distance, the gray tones recreate the original image. The specific appearance of the image is determined by the cutting direction and the fineness of the resolution. It is possible to mill in vertical, horizontal, concentric, and even fractal directions. The result is a relief that oscillates between abstract pattern and coherent image, depending on the viewing angle and distance. Because the image is easy to reproduce, the process is also suitable for large surfaces such as building façades and noise-protection walls. The maximum size of the panels is 2 x 4.90 m. Different materials such as wood, plastic, and concrete can be milled.[61]

Another technology based on visual abstraction is Ombrae. In this approach, parts of the surface are angled to reflect light in various directions. The desired image is built up from the interplay of light and shadow across the whole surface. Again, the first step here is to convert the image into gray values using a computer program. Special software calculates the optimal reflecting position of each individual pixel within the entire system. The finished image creates an astonishingly three-dimensional and almost holographic effect. As the viewer moves past the image, it too appears to move.

These "3D pixels" can be realized using a wide variety of materials. Metal, plastic, glass, concrete, paper, leather, and fabric can all be processed with computer technology. The size of the pixels can range from a few millimeters to several centimeters. Depending on the material, the structure can be punched, CNC milled, etched, or cast.[62]

61 — The 6 mm thick façade panels are processed with a special milling technology that enables the depiction of large-scale images. From close range, the composition of the overall image is not discernable and the surface exhibits an abstract texture. The panels are made of weatherproof material—a mixture of wood-based fibers compacted with thermosetting resins.
De Kleine Pijler Primary School, Rotterdam, 2008. Architecture: PLUS architecten, Rotterdam.

62 — Ombrae technology with "3D pixels" positioned at different angles. The shadows of the pixels are calculated so that they merge together and form an image when viewed from a distance.

A further "shadow material" that contains the information for multiple images in one and the same surface comes in the form of shadow casting panels (SCP). The basic idea here is that shadows are formed not only by the shape of a particular object, but also by the position of the light source. Under changing light scenarios, one and the same object can assume entirely different appearances. In neutral ambient light, the panels appear as a randomly arranged relief and no composition is discernable. But when illuminated from a particular side, they reveal one of the embedded images. The panels can either be made by hand using any chosen material or they can be 3D printed with computerized **selective laser sintering (SLS) technology.**[63]

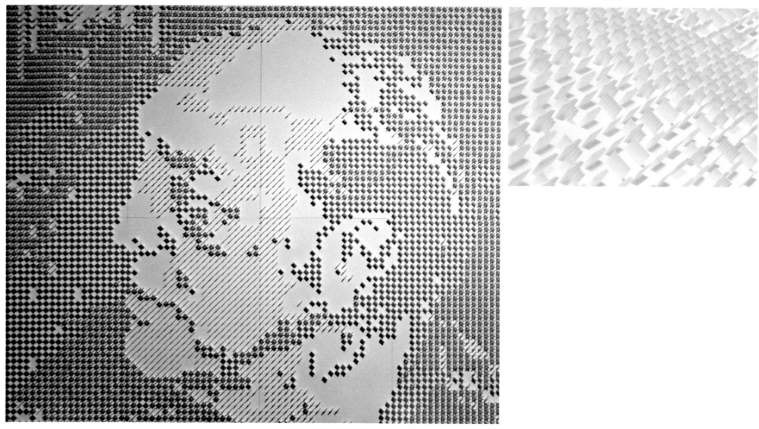

63 — Shadow-casting panels, which reveal different images in the same relief when the light source is varied. Design: Drzach & Suchy, Zurich.

Visual – Imaging

3.3 Ornamental

Beyond all the high-tech possibilities for manipulating material, there still remains a basic human need for surfaces that can be experienced on a sensory level. Away from the ever thinner, more effective, and barely visible functional coatings, a revival is currently taking place—back to conspicuous ornamentation, back to forms inspired by nature, and back to surfaces with a distinctive feel. Architecture and its translation into materials are not abstract concepts after all. Rather, they are about designing surfaces that reflect the aspirations of their users.

64 — Solid Poetry is a concrete surface with a special coating. If the surface is moistened with water, images appear that vanish when the surface dries out again. Design: Studio Molen, Frederik Molenschot & Susanne Happle, Zaandam.

65 — Walled paper: fine-cast wallpaper texture on glass-fiber-reinforced concrete panels that are just 8 mm thick.

66 — Concrete image that is first rasterized into bitmap dots and then rendered at high resolution using a surface treatment with retarding agent.

67 — CNC-lasered cowhide for upholstery or wall covering.

With ornamental treatment, materials can take on a completely new aura and identity. Even **concrete**, wich is considered hard and rational, can acquire a poetic quality using innovative techniques.

Apart from the familiar grain that is produced on concrete by wooden planks, a broad array of design possibilities is now opening up through the utilization of polyurethane synthetic molds. By inserting a negative mold into the formwork, relief-type structures can be created in the surfaces of site-mixed concrete as well as precast concrete components. The elastic properties of the material mean that even curves are easy to produce. Before the concreting process begins, the inserts must be fully adhered to the forms. The concrete quality also needs to be calibrated to suit the fineness of the patterning. With careful handling and the use of special release agents, the individual molds can be deployed up to a hundred times. Although a broad spectrum of ready-made patterns is available, the possibility of creating unique designs is a particularly interesting option here.[69]

Precise images can be produced by the partial roughening of surfaces. This can be done using methods such as hydroblasting or sandblasting. Another option with concrete is to slow down the setting process via a chemical reaction. The treated areas are later eluted. The difference between the rough, eluted areas and the otherwise smooth, intact concrete gives rise to the desired image. The exact method involves applying the chemical substance to a special film that retards the setting process in the coated areas. Self-compacting concrete is mostly used here as a prefabricated product in combination with a precise steel formwork. The depth of the eluted areas is normally one millimeter. Extremely accurate images can be created with this method—a photograph rasterized into bitmap dots can be realized in finished concrete with spaces of just 2 mm between the dots.[66, 70]

A special type of glass-fiber-reinforced fine-grained concrete makes it possible to create surfaces with an almost textile feel. The panels are just 8 mm thick and are produced using a hand-spray technique. Wallpaper is used as a mold and the liquid concrete mixture is sprayed on by hand using special applicators. The special cement is so fine that even highly detailed reliefs can be cast. The

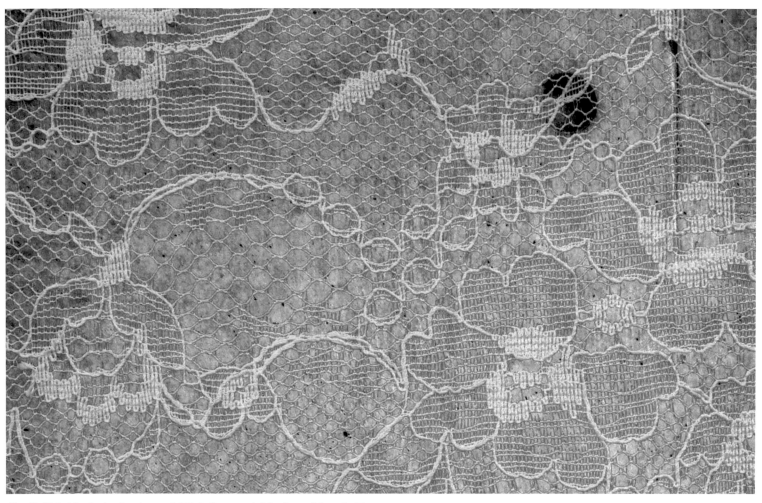

68 — Kochi Architects developed a special kind of ornamental "wallpaper" for a fashion store. Old and new surfaces are superimposed here without concealing one another. Both layers remain decipherable and the existing concrete with all its markings and blemishes was left untouched. This is covered with a semitransparent layer of fine lace fabric that was laminated onto the surface with liquid resin.
Adam et Rope, Tokyo, 2003. Architecture: Kazuyasu Kochi Studio, Tokyo.

"walled paper" panels can be fixed to existing walls and are deployable in both interior and exterior settings.[65]

Concrete slabs that react with water were developed as graduation work at the Design Academy Eindhoven. If the surface is moistened, patterns appear that are not visible when the material is dry. The idea is to develop hidden designs that are only revealed under certain conditions before vanishing again. The possible applications range from indoor features such as bathroom surfaces to outdoor usages like paving slabs with an integrated "rain effect."[64]

Apart from concrete, individual motifs can also be applied to any other material using techniques such as printing, milling, and embossing. Photorealistic images can be permanently rendered on glass surfaces, ceramics, plastics and even wood-product panels using special printing methods. With **CNC technology**, customized designs can be milled or cut into materials. There are hardly any technical limitations to the possibilities—from CNC-lasered hides to milled concrete reliefs.[67, 71]

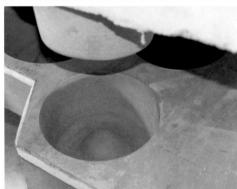

69— Enormous nubs measuring 16 cm in diameter and 8 cm in height dominate the appearance of this private art museum. To prevent visual gaps between the segments, the joints follow a zigzag line between the nubs. This made it crucial for the segments to be fabricated and fitted with millimeter-precise accuracy. The structures were produced using self-compacting concrete in polyurethane molds that measured 4 x 4 m. The release agent for this application was specially developed because the 420 nubs on each segment acted like suckers, making it hard to strip the formwork. PU structural molds can be used both for producing site-mixed concrete and manufacturing prefabricated components. Noppenhalle/Nubbed Building, Männedorf, 2007. Architecture: Baier Bischofberger GmbH, Zurich.

Visual – Ornamental

70 — Façade cladding made of "graphic concrete." The narrative ornamental designs are taken from historical documents stored in the archive.
Hämeenlinna Provincial Archives, Finland, 2009. Architecture: Heikkinen-Komonen Oy, Helsinki. Graphic design: Aimo Katajamäki, Helsinki.

71 — Graffiti artwork was the inspiration for the ornament that covers the surfaces on the ground floor of the residential complex. The same motif occurs in 2D and 3D versions. A gate serves as a spatial filter between the private space of the property and the public space of the sidewalk. It was cast from metal in reference to the New York tradition of cast iron architecture—except that the gate is made from cast aluminum rather than iron. The entire structure is more than 40 meters in length and was constructed from four different components that were initially designed using lifesize mockups of expanded polystyrene. The final pieces were fabricated using the traditional aluminum sand casting process, whereby molten aluminum is poured into a mold of bonded sand. This gives the surface a roughened, matte texture. Sand casting is also suitable for realizing complicated forms and undercuts with a high degree of technical sophistication, precision, and quality. The pattern on the sculptural gate is a recurring theme—appearing as an embossed feature in the surfaces of the stainless steel façade, providing a perforated cladding for the foyer ceiling, and milled into the oak panels of the reception area.
40 Bond Street, New York, 2006. Architecture: Herzog & de Meuron, Basel. Development of the metal ornaments: Exyd, Munich, Bo Gehring, New York.

Visual – Ornamental

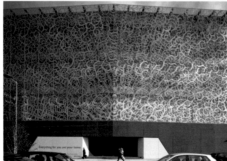

72 — An optical filter is created by two layers of glazing with printed ceramic frit patterns. Looking up at an oblique angle from the street below, the patterns are overlaid in such a way that the inside of the building is not visible from the outside. But when looking out from any of the retail floors, the patterns of the double façade are aligned to enable a direct view outwards through non-printed areas. Thus, all the floors are naturally lit even though the façade offers excellent privacy to the interior. The pattern on the external skin is mirroring and reflects the colors and shapes of the surroundings. This creates the overall impression of a three-dimensional fabric that varies in visual density and richness depending on the specific viewpoint, time of day, and light conditions.
John Lewis department store, Leicester, 2008. Architecture: Foreign Office Architects, London.

Glossary

Nanomaterials

Nanotechnology deals with structures in the range of 1–100 nm (nanometers).

One nanometer is defined as being one millionth of a millimeter. Nanoparticles with these dimensions exhibit special physical and chemical properties that differ from the equivalent solid matter. Nanotechnology is not a recent discovery. A wealth of particles on this scale can be found in nature—they are produced during combustion processes, for example. But what is new is that materials can now be manipulated on this level to change their functionality in meaningful ways. Materials can be nanostructured using a variety of methods. In the top-down approach, existing material is broken down to nanodimensions. In the bottom-up version, nanoparticles are constructed from even smaller atomic or molecular components.

Nanocoatings can be tailored to suit a specific purpose, equipping their substrates with a range of functional characteristics. They can be designed to counteract dirt, poor air quality, pollutants, graffiti, scratches, fingerprints, and bacteria—to name just a few examples.

Mechanical function
Ceramic or vitreous nanoparticles based on silicon oxide serve to protect surfaces against damage or scratches from mechanical wear. Special nanogel can be integrated as a transparent layer inside fire-protection glazing. In the event of fire, it expands and protects against the radiant heat of the blaze.

Cleaning function
With hydrophobic coatings, water forms into droplets that run off the surface and take impurities with them. Snti-graffiti coatings have extremely hydrophobic properties and can be applied as breathable sealings.

By contrast, hydrophilic layers cause the formation of a thin and evenly distributed film of water on the surface. This removes dirt particles by "scouring." Hydrophilic coatings with photocatalytic properties can even break down air pollutants using titanium dioxide (TiO_2) under the influence of UV radiation. Antibacterial surfaces can be manufactured with silver nanoparticles.

Optical function
The reflectivity of surfaces can be increased or reduced by the application of nanocoatings. This property is utilized by reflectors or optical glass. An anti-fog effect on windows or mirrors is produced by hydrophilic layers on which no droplets, but only an ultrathin film of water can form. The condensation is thus rendered inconspicuous.

—**page 118**

D
154 – 189

Powered Surfaces

1 — Façade study in which the tasks of a building envelope are performed by
functional films. The printed and laminated layers can generate electricity,
emit light, regulate the interior climate, and protect against the weather.
Smart Wrap™, Design: Kieran Timberlake, Philadelphia.

0.0 Materials in action

Materials are now becoming true performers. They can generate electricity, illuminate spaces, change their shape or color, and even absorb pollutants. "Smart" is the term often mentioned in this context. But do genuinely smart materials actually exist? Even the most innovative materials have never been animated with intelligence. The term "smart" refers instead to the property of being able to change state or appearance in response to external stimuli. Broadly speaking it refers to materials that exhibit active (or more precisely, reactive) behavior towards their surroundings. These reactions are initiated by the material itself and no electronic system is required to actuate the process. The state changes of the material are due entirely to its inherent properties or chemical composition. These functional innovations are more than just gimmicks. In future, they will make a decisive contribution to the efficiency of buildings—adapting to changing climate conditions, for example, or positively influencing the energy balance.

Energy-generating façades are a pioneering development towards a sustainable future of architecture in which energy is not simply consumed but also produced—ideally on a level that exceeds a building's own demand so that energy surpluses can be generated. The surfaces of the future will not simply aim to enhance the energy balance of individual buildings—they will be designed as part of larger energy networks. Energetic building products already exist that can be intelligently integrated within architectural concepts and are capable of meeting even sophisticated design criteria.

Energy-consuming building elements such as lighting are becoming extremely efficient due to new technologies. Furthermore, they can be integrated within surfaces. Light and surface thus merge into hybrid luminous materials that become an integral part of architectural elements such as the façade, interior walls, or furnishings. Electroluminescent light sources such as **LEDs** are highly efficient, durable, and robust, and their cold light enables them to be integrated within closed units such as façade panels. One of the biggest current light façades has recently been constructed in Beijing. It consists of innumerable LED "pixels" that illuminate the surface and turn it into a gigantic display screen measuring 2,200 m². But despite its enormous dimensions, the façade is a zero-energy system because the LEDs are powered at night by energy that is harvested during the day from the sun. The **solar cells** that generate this energy and the LEDs that consume the power are integrated within the façade.[16]

So even surfaces that initially appear to be relatively energy-intensive can actually be extremely efficient given the appropriate choice of technology. Here lies the fascination of active surfaces and "smart" materials—their character is multifaceted and there might be more beneath the surface than appears at first glance.

1.0 Energetic

1.1 Solar

Energy can be harnessed by photovoltaic surfaces that convert light into electricity. The **photovoltaic effect** was first recognized by Alexandre-Edmond Becquerel in 1839. It involves the release of positive and negative charge carriers upon exposure to light. In 1954, the first **silicon solar cells** were patented by Bell Laboratories in the U.S. Solar power is now gaining renewed attention against the backdrop of the current discussion on renewable energy sources. Neglected for many years due to an approach that had ecological ambition but lacked design acceptance, photovoltaics

2 — Photovoltaic modules with crystalline cell structure.

is experiencing something of a resurgence. This is largely due to new manufacturing technologies that make it possible to produce modules which can be integrated into the design and conceptual approach of sophisticated architecture. Photovoltaic panels can be installed on any roof and façade surface that receives sunlight. Depending on the size, positioning, and cell type of the photovoltaic surface, the system can—in ideal conditions—supply an entire household with electricity throughout the year, and even generate a surplus.

3 — Crystalline cells are extracted from the raw material silicon.

—**"Photovoltaics" page 188**

4 — Polycrystalline cells.

Solar cells consist of layers of semiconductors that generate direct current upon exposure to sunlight. Inverters then transform the direct current into alternating current before feeding the power into the electricity grid. The modules operate with no noise, zero emissions, and with a lifespan of between 20 and 30 years. Their effective-

5 — Monocrystalline cells integrated into laminated glass.

6 — Flexible a-Si thin-film coating on substrate foil.

7 — ETFE fluoropolymer membranes are increasingly deployed in translucent roofing. Manufactured using thin-film technology, PV (photovoltaic) film made of amorphous silicon can be laminated directly onto ETFE foil. Integrated within the roof, the energetic foil provides not only electricity but also shading.

8 — Electricity-generating polymeric membrane roofing as a prefabricated product with integrated thin-film technology.

ness is measured in terms of their conversion efficiency, which expresses how much of the absorbed solar energy is converted into electric current in percentage terms. With high-efficiency cells that utilize mirror and lens systems to concentrate greater light intensities onto the cells, maximum conversion efficiencies of around 40% are currently attainable.

A distinction is made between **crystalline cells** and **thin-film modules**. The contrasts lie in the differing appearance, manufacturing process, and conversion efficiency of the two forms. Most of the solar modules in current service are the crystalline cell type. These are based on the semiconducting material of silicon, which is found in abundant quantities in the Earth's crust. The silicon is cut into wafer-thin layers and then enclosed within protective coatings of glass or plastic. With the more recent thin-film modules, a semiconducting layer is deposited onto a rigid or flexible supporting substrate.

The conversion efficiency of crystalline cells ranges from around 14% to 20%. They are fabricated in layers approximately 0.2 mm thick. Individual solar cells are connected in series to form modules that have one positive and one negative terminal each. Based on different manufacturing methods, crystalline cells are themselves subdivided into monocrystalline cells with a smooth dark surface and polycrystalline cells with a randomly arranged and clearly visible cellular structure. To enhance their capacity for absorbing sunlight, the surfaces are given an anti-reflective treatment. The color of the crystalline modules depends on the thickness of this anti-reflective coating.[4, 5]

9 — The tiny elements flutter in the wind and enliven the building façade like leaves of ivy. On closer inspection, the artificial vegetation turns out to be an electricity-generating skin. A stainless-steel cable system is anchored to the façade to support the Solar Ivy leaf structures. Because it is composed of numerous small elements, the system can be optimally adapted to a wide variety of building shapes. Individual sections can be renewed as and when required, and the overall system can be extended without difficulty. The "leaves" consist of solar cells encapsulated in ETFE lamination. Solar Ivy. Design & development: Smit, New York.

greenish, and reddish depending on the manufacturing process. Conversion efficiencies of up to 12% are attainable depending on the material composition.[10-14]

Two different automated processes exist for the production of thin-film modules. The first is the continuous process for depositing photovoltaic materials onto rigid substrates such as glass. The second is the roll-to-roll method, which enables flexible substrates such as plastic or metal films to be coated.

The utilization of flexible substrate materials such as films is opening up new design possibilities. It means that transparent **ETFE** membrane roofs, polymeric roofing membranes, and solar-protection textiles can now be equipped with solar-active surfaces.[6-9, 19]

Thin-film modules are also available in the form of prefabricated façade systems. Frameless modules can even be adhered to backing panels and used as cladding in ventilated façade systems. This produces a very smooth and homogenous overall appearance. The wiring is housed out of sight in the space between the layers. The elements are delivered to the construction site ready to install—they simply need to be fitted into the substructure and connected up. When covered with translucent colored glazing, these modules are available in red, green, yellow, blue, and white.[12]

Thin-film modules can be made of amorphous silicon (a-Si), copper indium diselenide (CIS) or cadmium telluride (CdTe). The coating thickness of these semiconducting materials is measured in terms of microns. Thin-film modules also perform relatively well in diffuse lighting conditions. Their surface appears dark, almost black with a subtle trace of color that varies between bluish,

12 — Ventilated façade system with frameless panels. The modules are glued directly onto a façade panel. Colored translucent cover glazing makes the frameless elements an interesting option for innovative design projects. The modules are available in the dimensions 60 x 120 cm.

10 — SurPLUShome—Darmstadt University of Technology's winning entry to the Solar Decathlon 2009 international university competition—is a prototype residential house. In order to reduce overall energy consumption, the envelope is insulated as effectively as possible with vacuum insulation, phase-change material, and triple glazing. The roof and façade are fitted with photovoltaic elements. On the façade, thin-film modules provide a homogenous, shingle-type skin that extends around the entire building. The architectural integration of photovoltaics thus gives rise to an elegant and contemporary design.
SurPLUShome, 2009. Design & development: Darmstadt University of Technology (TU Darmstadt), Unit of Energy-Efficient Building Design, Prof. Manfred Hegger.

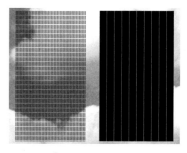

13 — Solar modules with screen-printed color coatings. The dot screens cover part of the active surface but cause no significant reduction in performance. PVACCEPT, La Spezia, 2004. Design: Ingrid Hermannsdörfer, Prof. Ingo F. Schneider (process is protected by patent).

14 — Thin-film modules that serve as combined shading and photovoltaic elements.

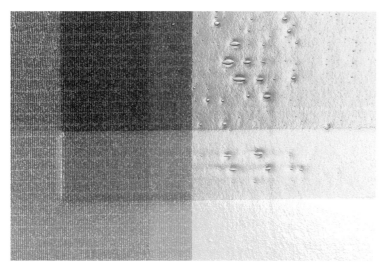

11 — Float glass, textured glass, and fused colored glass are combined with thin-film modules to create a visually appealing composite. The power-generating façade can thus be transformed into a work of art.

15 — Flexible organic photovoltaic cells can be produced using the inexpensive roll-to-roll manufacturing process.

16 — Greenpix: zero-energy light façade with around 2,300 LEDs that provide colored backlighting to the façade's solar modules—the exact same modules that power the LEDs. The daily solar yield varies depending on the weather conditions and is reflected in the display's lighting intensity at night. The illumination is soft after periods of fog, but sunny days are followed by intense brightness at night.
Xicui Entertainment Center, Beijing, 2007. Architecture: Simone Giostra & Partners, New York. Engineers: Ove Arup & Partners, London/ Beijing.

17 — A lighting system for streets and public squares. The energy required at night for the LEDs radiating downwards is generated during the day by the photovoltaic panels attached to the top of the lamps and stored in batteries. The Solar Tree can bridge up to three consecutive days without sunshine.
Solar Tree. Design: Ross Lovegrove, London.

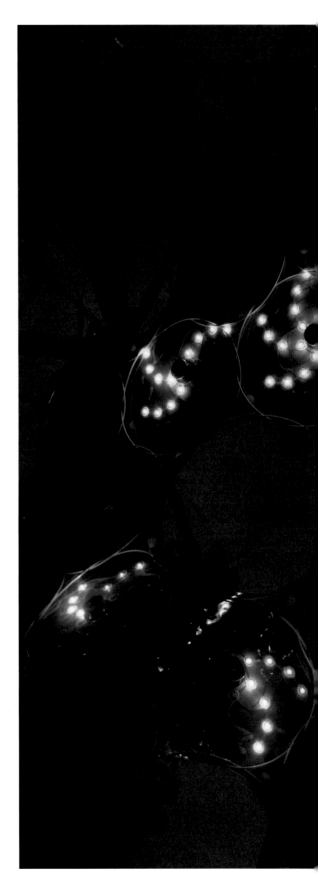

18 — Metabolic Media consists of a web of geo-textile structures and solar cells designed to charge the batteries of a pump system that waters and monitors plants growing on a mesh and providing berries or fruit. The architects explored the mechanism of dye-sensitized solar cells that mimic the process of photosynthesis in green plants, using dye rather than chlorophyll to absorb energy from light. A modular photovoltaic membrane was prototyped to provide support for the plants, shelter and shade from the sun during the day, and light using LEDs with printed circuitry at night.
Metabolic Media, 2008. Design: Loop.pH, London, in collaboration with Risø DTU, the National Laboratory for Sustainable Energy, Denmark.

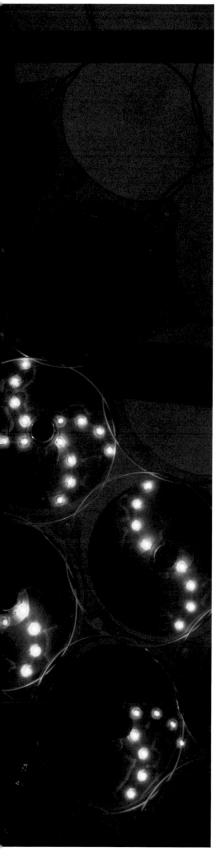

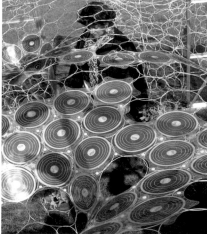

19 — The aim of Portable Light is to make existing semiconductor technologies accessible to large numbers of people who would otherwise be living without electricity. A textile material that can be fabricated with traditional weaving techniques is fitted with a flexible energy-generating PV film and LEDs that provide white light. Produced as portable bags, these units can be taken anywhere and recharged during the day. They can even be used to recharge cell phones and other electrical devices. When night falls, individual units can be deployed as reading lights or several units can be interconnected to provide illumination for larger gatherings. A 4 watt solar textile unit weighs around 340 grams, takes 3 hours to charge, and can supply 8 hours of light. One particularly compelling aspect of this project is the transfer of high-tech materials—manufacturable at low cost in large quantities and easy to handle—to a low-tech setting. Quality of life is improved via simple means that fit into existing socio-cultural environments.
Portable Light, 2005. Design & development: KVA MATx, Kennedy and Violich Architecture, Boston.

Energetic – Solar

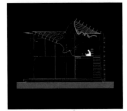  

20 —The traditional solid wall is challenged here by soft textiles with flexible organic solar cells and LEDs woven in. Movable energy-harvesting curtains are used to both shade the house and divide up space. At the same time, these textiles can supply around 50% of the power required by an average household in the U.S. Integrated into the skylight is a central curtain that can be lowered to create an instant space or folded upwards to serve as a luminous fabric chandelier. Power-generating surfaces are thus an integral feature of the building's overall design concept.
Soft House, 2007–2009. Architecture & development: KVA MATx, Kennedy and Violich Architecture, Boston.

With organic solar cells, sunlight is converted into voltage based on conducting polymers using a semiconducting nanocomposite. The cells can be "printed" onto flexible substrates using the roll-to-roll method, which is similar to conventional mass-production operations such as newspaper printing. This makes them extremely low-cost and efficient to manufacture. The flexible cells can also be used to provide everyday objects with effective solar energy. It would thus be inexpensive to produce electricity-generating awnings, tents, and clothing. But work is still being done to improve the conversion efficiency of organic solar cells, which is currently around just 3%.[15, 20]

1.2 Piezoelectric

Surfaces that convert movement into electric power can be realized with piezoelectric elements. Piezoelectricity is the generation of voltage when material is deformed. This natural phenomenon can be observed with ceramics, crystals, and polymers, and the principle is already used in sensors and switches. As a research project, a flooring system was recently developed that utilizes impact kinetic energy from human movement. The floor tiles can be installed in any public space where large volumes of people circulate—train stations, sports stadiums, and nightclubs are suitable venues. The system can also harness energy from vehicular traffic in parking garages and drive-thrus. Furthermore, the

Glass surfaces can also be color-designed with screen printing, whereby a maximum of 10% to 20% of the surface is covered by a fine ceramic dot screen. Although no photovoltaic activity takes place on the printed spots, the relatively small proportion of printed area means that the conversion efficiency of the overall module is barely affected. This method can be used to equip signs and guidance systems with electricity-generating capability.[13]

Thin-film modules on a rigid supporting material can also be designed as semitransparent solar protection elements. Parts of the layers can be milled, scored, or laser cut to give the modules up to 50% transparency.[14]

One relatively new development in solar energy is **organic solar cells** and **dye solar cells**. These require even less material to produce and are particularly low-cost. Dye solar cells convert sunlight into electricity using a dye solution. The technology even works under weak lighting conditions such as indoor settings. It offers new design possibilities because the modules are semitransparent and can be manufactured via screen printing. The cells are highly fragile and need to be protected with glass panels.

21 — The piezoelectric flooring surface generates electricity from kinetic energy and can be deployed wherever large volumes of people are in motion.
Powerleap, 2008. Design & development: Elisabeth Redmond, Andrew Katz.

flooring surface can relay information about its utilization to intelligent traffic control systems. The tiles activate small piezoceramic plates that have a brass reinforcement shim and are covered with nickel electrodes. When these plates are bent, a charge is induced sufficient to illuminate embedded LEDs. Although the system is only capable of low amounts of power output at this stage, it is helping to draw attention to the potential of harnessing energy from humans.[21]

2.0 Illuminated

Building equipment is increasingly being integrated into interior surfaces. This also applies to artificial light, which serves as a fundamental design element in setting the tone of a particular space and creating the desired ambience. The walls themselves are now beginning to glow. Light sources are no longer confined to lamps and light fixtures.

The key technology lies with so-called "luminescent" materials that are breaking new ground in the sphere of functional light design. Entire surfaces can be activated as homogenously luminous light sources. Unlike the almost obsolete light bulb that converts most of its energy into heat and only a small fraction into light, luminescent materials with their cold light translate the energy supply into visible light with almost no loss. In other words, they are considerably more efficient. **Luminescence** refers to the optical radiance that can be stimulated either by electric current (electroluminescence) or light exposure (photoluminescence).

22 — LED light is reflected on the stainless-steel mesh. Tubes are again fitted here with LEDs, but in this case they are installed a slight distance from the façade and direct the light back towards the mesh.

2.1 Luminescent

Electroluminescent

Electroluminescent technology provides the basis for light-emitting diodes (LEDs), organic light-emitting diodes (OLEDs), and electroluminescent films (EL films).

An **LED** consists of two electrodes (anode and cathode) plus a semiconductor that serves as the luminescent material and produces light in a specific color. The color depends on the utilized semiconductor material. The first color LEDs appeared on the market in the 1960s and their efficiency and color spectrum have

been improving ever since. But only since 1995 has it been possible to manufacture the white light required in most applications because the technology needs to be fabricated with a special process. The light yield from white LEDs has now reached the level of light bulbs.

23 — A see-through media façade covering the entire building envelope can be realized using a stainless steel mesh with integrated color LEDs. Visibility from the building interior to the outside is retained. Tubes are incorporated at regular intervals within the mesh to hold the light-emitting diodes in a permanent and waterproof housing. The façade is computer-controllable and can depict images.

LEDs have long lifespans of up to 100,000 hours because they have no wearing parts such as filaments. Due to the coldness of their light, there is no need for ventilation or heat abstraction. Furthermore, their small size and resistance to impact and vibration mean that LEDs can be permanently embedded in materials. This makes them ideal for closed or sealed units, allowing LEDs to be deployed as "light pixels" for displaying changing images or low-resolution film sequences within computer-controlled lighting systems.

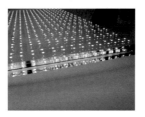

24 — Laminated glazing in which light-emitting diodes (LEDs) are integrated and wirelessly supplied with electricity.

Light-emitting diodes almost seem to coalesce with their surroundings when they are embedded within multilayer glass that is electrified by conductive coatings. The points of light appear to float in the glass and can be individually activated. This kind of hybrid material system can be used to integrate features such as lighting and signage systems within architectural elements like transparent partitions and railings.[24]

The color version of apparently light-emitting glass is fed with colored LED light from the edges of the panel. The glass surface is printed with a fine white dot screen and each dot acts as a deliberate "impurity," coupling the light out of the panel in a controlled manner and thus appearing in the same color as the light. The red, green, and blue (RGB) LEDs can be controlled using computer software to make them illuminate in changing color sequences and light compositions.[25]

OLEDs represent an entirely new type of illumination. Based on extremely thin layers of conductive polymers, their light color is chemically determined within the polymer structure. Their lifespan is 10 times longer than conventional light bulbs and again they do not warm up. OLEDs are considered the light technology of the future because they can be used to produce flat-light

25 — A ceramic dot screen covers around 10% of the glass surface. The dots couple out the colored light that is fed into the side, thus appearing the same color as the light. This results in a harmonious lighting effect, the color of which can be dynamically changed. Equipped with RGB LEDs, the panels can emit light in the entire color spectrum.

26 — Transparent roof tiles with integrated LEDs. During the day, the system uses solar cells to absorb energy. This energy is then used to power the roof at night, illuminating static or moving images and advertising messages. The roof tiles act here as gigantic "pixels." Light Emitting Roof Tiles. Design & development: Lambert Kamps, Groningen.

sources of high quality. At this point in their development, they are still sensitive to moisture and oxygen, currently making it necessary to encapsulate them behind glass. With a total thickness of just 1.5 mm, the elements can easily be integrated within existing units or layers of material. The luminance of the evenly radiant surface depends on the light color, but can reach up to 1,000 cd/m². [28, 29]

In contrast, the luminance of electroluminescent films is relatively low. But the advantage here is that they can be cut into the required shape with scissors or cutters. They are fabricated in any length "off the roll" using a printing method. The luminous component is a zinc sulfide powder embedded between two electrodes. The light produced by **EL films** is non-flickering and non-dazzling, and can be emitted in various colors. With lifespans of at least 10,000 hours, these thin and bendable films are ideal for backlighting and emergency lighting applications.[35]

Numerous designers have already begun investigating the creative possibilities of electroluminescent surfaces. The main focus of attention here is on the easily processable EL films.

The Dutch designer Jonas Samson has developed an **electroluminescent wallpaper** prototype. By activating individual seg-

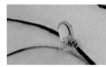

27 — In the LED-x light prototype, <u>carbon fibers</u> stitched onto a textile backing not only provide the supporting structure but also act as electricity conductors. Two threads insulated from one another form an electric circuit and operate as electricity-conducting paths. At the intersection points of the threads, LEDs are simply attached to resin that was made conductive by mixing carbon powder into the liquid plastic. Design & Development: Gerd Falk, Stuttgart.

28 — Organic light-emitting diode (OLED).

29 — The OLEDs are enclosed within a transparent film and combined to create a flexible light surface. The technical components and wiring are visible and part of the design. Design: Ingo Maurer, Munich.

ments in sequence with the help of a computer program, the pattern can expand or shrink. The wallpaper itself consists of two layers—electroluminescent film underneath, with a layer of paper on top to create the visual and textural impression of generic wallpaper. If the lighting function is not activated, it looks like a common wallpapered surface. But with the light, it suddenly comes alive. Brightness and color can be varied to suit requirements, and the interactive wallpaper can even display simple animations.[33]

The designers at Loop.pH in London have been experimenting with different sensors that control lighting. This enables the illumination process to be triggered by events in the immediate surroundings. The material thus appears to be responding to its environment.[32, 34]

With the Blumen Wallpaper project, they designed light-kinetic partition elements whose patterning and light intensity can be individually adapted to different spatial functions and lighting conditions. The pattern is printed onto a textile using electroluminescent ink. Rather than concealing the electric wiring, it is deliberately emphasized as part of the design and is ornamentally integrated within the surface. One interesting aspect of this project is the contrast between the high-tech electronics and the traditional floral pattern that is recontextualized through its repetitive appearance and its interaction with the technology. A flexible software program enables the parameters for the lighting's duration and brightness to be adapted to the setting.[36]

In Santiago Calatrava's auditorium for the Valencia Opera House, furnishings and light merge together. The architect deployed electroluminescent film integrated within the seating's satin glass panels as background lighting for the space. The brightness of these luminous elements can be varied and calibrated with the overall lighting concept to create the desired atmosphere. Furthermore, the special seat panels act as emergency lighting. [37]

30 — Digital Dawn: electroluminescent window blind. Design: Loop.pH, London.

Illuminated – Luminescent

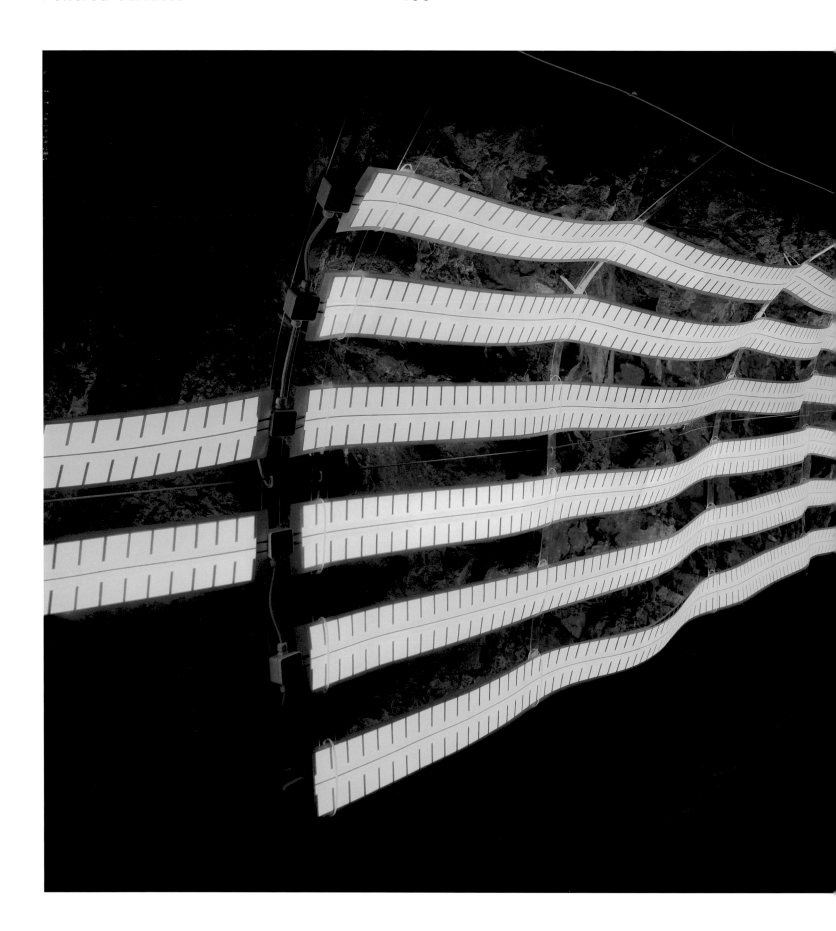

31 — The illuminated box was placed in a public park as a temporary installation. One could enter the fully lit tunnel at night. The geometrical and technological atmosphere stood in strong contrast to the darkness of the surrounding park. At night, the solar panels that covered the walls transmitted the stored energy to the luminescent wall panels, which brightly illuminated the pavilion.
Boxenstop. Braunschweig, 2000. Design: Daniel Hausig, Hamburg.

For an art event, lighting bands made of electroluminescent foil were attached to a specially installed intermediate current meter in a former mining gallery, tapping an amount of energy so small that it can neither be recorded nor subsequently charged. The title, Stromdiebstahl [Energy Theft] refers to a legal discussion that came up in the late 19th century and questioned whether energy can be a tangible good in the first place.
Stromdiebstahl, Installation, Osnabrück, 2001. Design: Daniel Hausig, Hamburg.

Illuminated – Luminescent

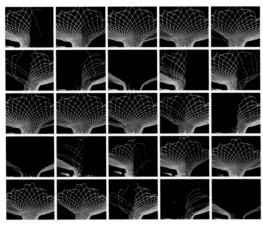

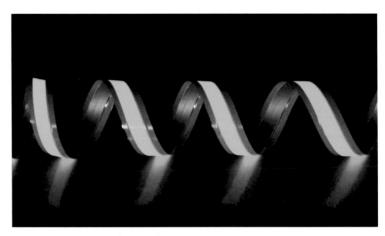

32 — In the Sonumbra project, an umbrella structure in a public park interacts with noises from its surroundings and transforms them into light signals. The canopy is made of an electroluminescent mesh that is activated by electrical impulses from microphones in the immediate environment. This causes the mesh to light up. Activity in the surrounding area is thus visualized as an optical rhythm. Sonumbra. Design: Loop.pH, London.

35 — Electroluminescent film (EL film).

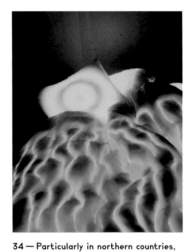

36 — Electroluminescent ink is used to print ornamental designs onto fabric. These designs can be activated in varying segments to form ever-changing structures that respond to the environment via sensors. The wiring for the electricity supply is not concealed, but is used as an integral part of the ornamental concept. Blumen Wallpaper. Design: Loop.pH, London.

34 — Particularly in northern countries, the chronic lack of light in the winter months can lead to serious health issues such as depression. This phenomenon is known as seasonal affective disorder (SAD). Luminous bedding with electroluminescent threads can help to bring light into the darkness here. To give the biological body clock a better chance of coping, the duvet and pillow simulate a natural dawn. The result is a gentler alternative to the conventional alarm clock—the high-tech bedding gradually starts to glow at a specified time, getting steadily brighter over a 15–20 minute period. Waking up thus becomes more of a natural process. Light Sleeper. Design: Loop.pH, London.

33 — Electroluminescent wallpaper capable of producing moving images on a paper surface. When switched off, the surface reveals nothing of its luminous potential. Light Emitting Wallpaper. Design: Jonas Samson, Utrecht.

37 — The more than 4,000 seats of the Opera House are fitted with electroluminescent side panels that can be controlled via computer software. Their light intensity is adjusted to suit the different functions within the auditorium—from emergency lighting to concert mode. El Palau de Les Arts Reina Sofìa, Valencia. Architecture: Studio Santiago Calatrava, Zurich. Furniture design: Studio Santiago Calatrava with Poltrona Frau, Torino.

Photoluminescent

Photoluminescent surfaces are excited into a luminous state by exposure to light. They are categorized into two main groups—**fluorescent** and **phosphorescent** materials. With fluorescent materials, the luminous effect stops as soon as the external light source is discontinued, while phosphorescent materials continue to glow for hours. Phosphorescent materials are fabricated by adding special pigments that vary in terms of their color, intensity, and duration of luminescence. These additives can be integrated within plastics and fabrics as well as artificial stone and solid surface materials.

Beyond its visual effect, photoluminescence also has some quite practical functions. Phosphorescent surfaces can be used as emergency lighting, glowing for up to 12 hours after a power blackout.[39]

The design studio gruppe RE has developed an afterglowing glass tile. Thanks to the phosphorescent properties of its glass-ceramic coating, the tile changes color and appearance from day to night. Superior color depth and brilliance are achieved by back-coating the glass surface.[40]

39 — This luminous resin-based solid surface has a warm white color in daylight, turning to a cool green glow in the dark. The thermoformable and flame-retardant material is available in sheets or strips. It continues to work as emergency lighting even after the power supply has been cut off. Deployed as regular night lighting, the material helps to save energy.

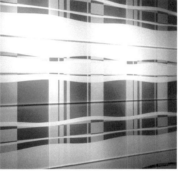

A visual interplay of emerging and fading luminous patterns was explored by Kennedy & Violich Architects in New York with their Give Back Curtains. These fabrics require no power supply—they harvest natural light during the day, "recycle" it with photoluminescent pigments, and then release it with a time delay. Pigments with different colors and varying excitation and afterglow phases are deployed here. Weaving them together produces a dynamic pattern that continues to evolve throughout the night.[41]

38 — Photoluminescent waterproof protective clothing for nighttime outdoor activities.

40 — Glass with afterglow effect. A glass-ceramic coating with phosphorescent properties is fired into the surface as vitreous enamel. Excitation from natural or artificial light is enough to produce an afterglow of up to 10 hours. The material is produced in panel sizes of 2 x 4 m.

41 — Floor-to-ceiling photoluminescent curtains can be used to provide flexible partitioning for temporary spaces. As dynamic design elements, they generate different colors and patterns over a period of several hours. Natural and artificial light are harvested during the day and then released over varying periods of time by threads with different pigmentations, resulting in permanently evolving patterns of color. Give Back Curtains. Design & development: KVA MATx, Kennedy and Violich Architecture, Boston.

D — 2.2

42 — Created for the Tokyo Fiber Exhibition, the bench
designed by Gwenael Nicolas appears to be woven from
light. The coarse mesh of the seating surface consists of
180 flexible light-transmitting synthetic fibers measuring
1 mm in diameter. If the fibers are bent through a small
radius, their internal reflection changes and light is also
emitted along the sides. Sensors control the light intensity
and respond to human movement. When approached, the
bench starts to glow.
Mist Bench, 2009. Design: Gwenael Nicolas, Tokyo.

2.2 Light-transmitting

Light-transmitting materials are not luminous themselves—they simply distribute or transport light. But they do this over distances that can span entire buildings. Sunlight can thus be guided via light transmission into the inner sections of building complexes that would otherwise receive no natural daylight.

Used in fiber-optic cables for telecommunication, **glass fibers** are known to be excellent light transmitters. Electric signals are converted here into light signals for transmission purposes. Fiber-optic cables are sheathed in a housing that causes total internal reflection, allowing light waves to be transmitted with almost no loss. In addition to being ideal for sending information, this property can also be utilized for transporting light to different parts of a building or through solid materials. Optical light-transmitting fibers are manufactured from glass or plastic.[43, 44]

43 — Light-transmitting synthetic fibers.

44 — Fiber optics serve to guide natural light deep into the interior of large office buildings. Unlike conventional daylight distribution systems, the fiber-optic strands are threaded through floors and ceilings to create lofted interior volumes. If the strands are cut off below the ceiling, they can be used to form a type of chandelier. The strands can be illuminated at night by the stored solar energy.
Fiber Optic Room, 2006. Architecture: IwamotoScott, ISAR, San Francisco.

If **light-transmitting fibers** are embedded within solid building materials such as **concrete**, the material can be backlit to produce highly aesthetic effects on the surface. Extremely small proportions of glass fiber (around 4%) are enough to make fine-grained concrete appear almost entirely translucent when illuminated from behind. But despite the resulting ethereal impression, the concrete exhibits outstanding material strength. Shadows cast on the rear side of the material show through on the front with incredible precision. Solid load-bearing concrete walls thus acquire the transparency of paper. This fascinating contrast between solidity and translucence turned the material into an overnight sensation when it first appeared. Originally developed for a research project, the material is now available as a commercial building product. Prefabricated room-high panels with average thicknesses of 2–3 cm are available, but blocks with thicknesses of up to 50 cm can also be produced.[48]

Further variants now include 15 cm thick prefabricated wall sections with an insulating core. These sections can also be deployed as exterior building elements. And if cut extremely thin, the light-transmitting concrete is transformed into a

45 — Light-transmitting concrete veneer that is suitable for high-quality surfaces in building, automobile, or yacht interiors.

veneer that can be laminated onto transparent substrates for building, automobile and yacht interiors.[45]

If light-transmitting fibers are arranged in a dense grid, they can be used as a display for pixelated images via rear projection. In the prototype developed by the designer Christoffer Dupont, the synthetic fibers have a diameter of 1 mm and are positioned with grid spacing of just 1.15 mm. This principle enables concrete surfaces to be transformed into digital signage or information panels.[46]

Solid blocks of plastic can also be made to transmit light by applying a special milling technique to the interior. Light entering the crystal-clear **acrylic glass** (PMMA) is then routed along light-transmitting edges so that the transparent material seems to glow from within. Light, shadow, and color appear in unexpected patterns on the surface.[47]

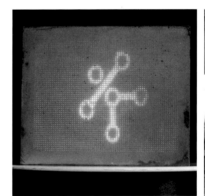

46 — Optical fibers are embedded in concrete in a grid formation, enabling them to serve as pixels for a "concrete screen." Projectors situated behind the surface act as light sources, sending moving images through the solid concrete to appear on the façade.
Design & development: Christoffer Dupont, Copenhagen.

47 — Light-transmitting synthetic blocks made of acrylic glass.

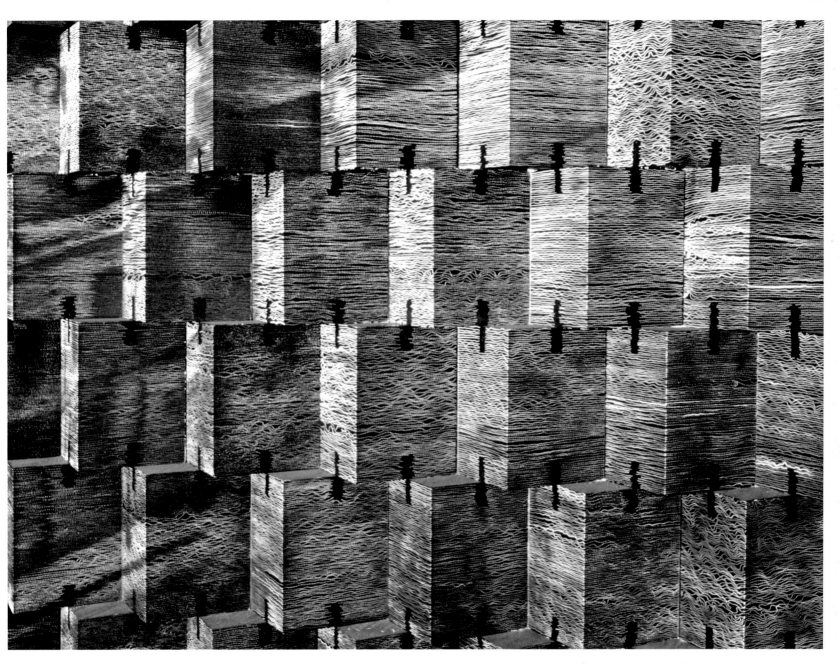

48 — Optical fibers can be embedded in concrete. If the material is cut into blocks, light-transmitting "bricks" are produced with a unique aesthetic. The light appears to flow right through the concrete.
Tokyo Fiber '09 – Senseware. Design: Kengo Kuma & Associates, Tokyo.

3.0 Responsive

Building surfaces that respond to their surroundings can adapt in highly specific ways to architectural requirements. Sensors integrated within materials can monitor weather conditions and activate solar, rain, or wind protection. Intelligent flooring surfaces can provide data about the circulation of people in a building, triggering dynamic signage systems as required. Information can be collected and evaluated. Looking beyond the Big Brother aspect, this approach can be utilized to implement extremely practical applications such as localized alarm or emergency systems. —**"Smart Materials" page 188**

3.1 Information-transmitting

Fabrics and textiles represent an interesting field for new responsive materials because weaving technology makes it easy to integrate functional components into "**smart textiles**." Furthermore, systems of "wearable computing" can monitor and transmit specific data. The main force driving innovation here is the military—soldiers in action need to avoid the restriction of having to carry and handle cumbersome devices. User interfaces can be woven directly into clothing, making them easier to access and operate. Meanwhile, body-hugging textiles can transmit information about the wearer's physical condition, enabling injured persons to get assistance in the event of an emergency. Sensors embedded in "smart shirts" monitor the physical condition, ECG, breathing, and fluid balance of the wearer. Thus, a shirt is no longer simply a piece of clothing but can now be a wearable biometric data surface. Beneficial civilian applications also exist in sports and medical technology.

Electronic textiles ("**e-textiles**") sense how and where they are being touched and can respond to the pressure signal. The technology is able to differentiate between simple presses, swipes, and gestures, interpreting the information accordingly. E-textiles are woven from electrically-conductive fibers or yarns, thus dispensing with the need for conventional wiring. Their functioning principle is based on the layering of conductive textile with insulating fabric in between. If a specific area is touched, the layers are compressed together to close an electric circuit and the point of contact is localized by the position of x and y values in the textile. Control units then translate the signal into a command for the connected electronic devices. This technology has countless po-

49 — E-textiles can localize pressure signals via the positional x and y values of the conductive fibers within the fabric. The resulting data can be evaluated to control electronic devices.

50 — Conductive yarns transform switching on the lights into a sensual experience. Touching the soft fuzzy surface will turn the lights on and off or simply dim them, depending on the type of contact. The control signals are transmitted by the yarns themselves—no buttons are hidden inside.
Essential Square Wall Dimmer, 2008. Design & development: International Fashion Machines (IFM), Seattle.

tential applications—from sports clothing with interwoven control panels for cell phones or iPods, to sofas with remote controls integrated into the covers, to the monitoring of occupied seats in public assembly spaces.[49]

An "**intelligent**" **carpet** that can recognize if and where it is being walked over—and will transmit the collected information—is no longer a futuristic idea either. This product was originally developed for room monitoring, but it has the potential to become an integral feature in building technology. The carpet can be linked up with the climate-control system or used as an interactive guidance system with the help of integrated LEDs. It can be fitted with sensors to monitor vibration, pressure, and temperature.

A network of microchips relays the information to an evaluation unit, and intelligent software solutions analyze the signals for specific tasks. Thus, an alarm signal can be triggered if the system recognizes a path of movement towards a particular window or emergency exit. Security zones can be individually defined and changed at different times of day. Carpet sensors can also be deployed as automatic door openers, light switches, and people counters.

Furthermore, different sensory functions (pressure, temperature, and movement) combined in monitoring systems for private households can detect someone lying motionless on the floor and can send out a distress call. The Thinking Carpet can thus be a genuine lifesaver for people in need of assistance after a bad fall, for instance.[51]

Another example of an intelligent surface based on sensor technology was on show in the Spanish pavilion at the World Expo 2008 in Zaragoza. Visitors left traces of light on this material—their steps were magically preserved in the floor as footprints that began to fade after a few seconds and then completely disappeared. The floor could thus "remember" the user. The underlying technology here is based on a networked system of **electroca-**

51 — Even carpet can be deployed for room monitoring: Sensors provide information about the type and intensity of movements in the space, and the carpet can be linked to guidance systems or alarm installations if required. The layer of sensors is placed under the actual pile fabric and invisible to the user.

52 — When approached, the surface responds by illuminating so that the user's movements are captured on the surface.

pacitive sensors. When objects or humans approach, the sensors detect a change in the electrostatic field of their surroundings and relay this information to a programmable timer that controls the **LEDs** integrated in the module. The duration and intensity of the timer can be adjusted so that different scenarios are possible. If the sensors are activated, the lights can be made to appear and fade quickly or slowly. They can illuminate permanently after a single approach or they can become brighter and more intense with each successive movement. In theory, the size of the total light surface is unlimited. The individual modules measure 15 x 15 cm and each contain 36 LEDs.

Large contiguous surfaces can be installed by simply plugging the individual parts together on site. The modules start responding to approaching objects from a distance of 15 cm—the surface does not actually need to be touched for the lighting to react. Installed as an interactive wall, the technology can be illuminated with a wave of the hand. But the capacitive sensors can be connected to more than just LEDs. Via an external computer, other functions such as acoustic responses and alarms can also be activated when someone approaches or touches the surface. It is also possible for specific patterns and images to be displayed on the entire surface when people draw near.[52]

3.2 Color-changing

For the visual design of surfaces, materials that can change their appearance are an interesting option. Chameleon-like surfaces capable of adapting their color exert a fascination. These "chromogenic" materials respond to changes in ambient temperature, lighting conditions, and electric current. Photochromic materials react upon exposure to UV light. Thermochromic materials change their color with the temperature. **Electrochromic coatings** modify their appearance when voltage is applied **(cf. Chapter 3, Adaptive Layers). Photochromic and thermochromic pigments** can be incorporated within paints or plastic materials that are suitable for coating interior surfaces. Applications for exterior settings have so far remained unsuccessful due to the poor UV resistance and durability of the materials.

Photochromic systems change from transparent to colored or switch from one color to another upon exposure to UV light. Self-darkening sunglasses belong to this category of materials. Surfaces that respond to light can thus indicate the intensity of solar radiation. Originating from a collaboration between designers and architects, Orproject deploys photoreactive material on an architectural scale. In shaded conditions, the polygonal segments of the curved surface are white. But when hit by sunlight, they turn an intense blue color. The surface keeps changing throughout the day with constantly varying tones.[60]

53 — Thermochromic polymer film with reversible switching between blue and colorless. Color-changing components can be incorporated within a polymer matrix, thereby enabling them to withstand the production process for synthetic materials (vacuum forming, extrusion, etc.). Development: Fraunhofer Institute for Applied Polymer Research, Potsdam.

Thermochromic surfaces change their color in response to changes in the ambient temperature—either by turning from one color to another or from colored to colorless. The temperature at which the color change occurs can be individually calibrated to the specific purpose. Color-changing pigments were originally used in the field of automobile development to indicate engine parts that had overheated. Thermochromic products in everyday life currently include fever-indicating films and storage-temperature indicators on sensitive goods (e.g. in medical technology).[53-54, 56-58]

Researchers at Keio University in Japan have developed a chameleon-like thermochromic fabric module with conductive yarns that can change its color to red, green, or blue when voltage is applied (thereby warming it up). This enables the color of apparel to

Responsive – Color-changing

54 — Electronic textiles (e-textiles) are innovative materials that incorporate conductive fibers directly into the textile itself. These materials eliminate wires and hard electronics and have a soft tactile feel. Woven conductive yarns heat up when activated. If thermochromatic ink is partially applied to the yarns of the double weave, one and the same fabric takes on different color patterns that can be controlled by a special computer software.
Moving Target & Running Plaid, 2007, Design Maggie Orth, International Fashion Machines Inc., Seattle.

D — 3.2

Responsive – Color-changing

55 — The prototype of the E-Static Shadows installation consists of an e-textile system that responds to electrostatic charges. If visitors stroke the surface with their clothing, hands, or hair, the resulting electrostatic charge is visualized by switching off the integrated LEDs wherever the electrical membrane detects the charge. This results in dynamic shadow patterns that reflect the activities in the space. The e-textile prototype consists of woven sensors using computer-aided Jacquard weaving, polyester and conductive threads, LEDs, transistors, and power supply.
E-Static Shadows. Design & development: Prof. Zane Berzina, London.

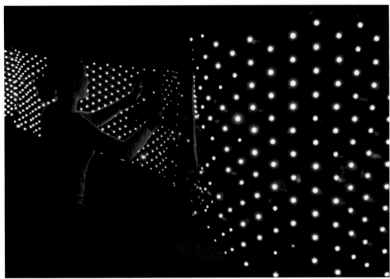

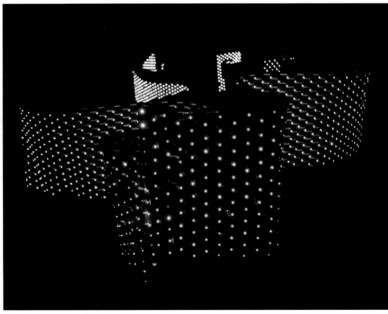

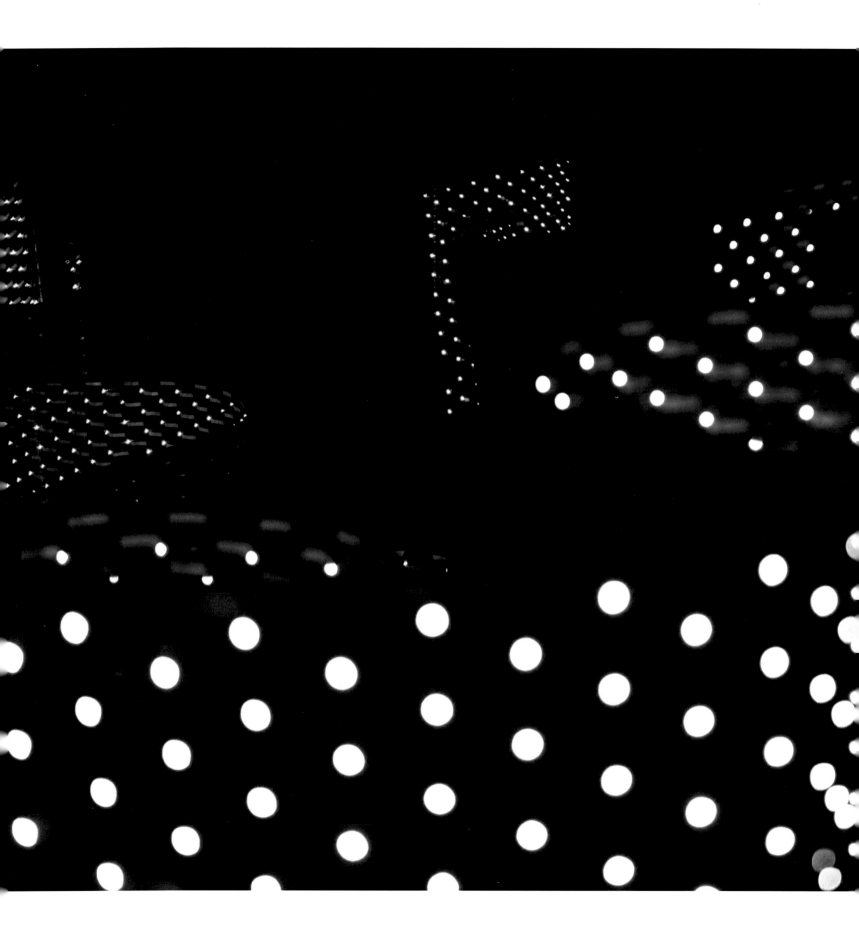

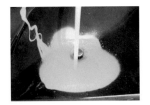

56 — Washbasin with thermo-chromic coating.

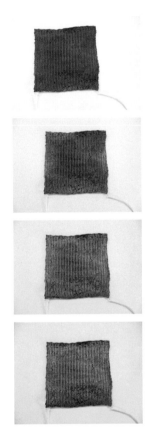

57 — Chameleon-like textile that is interwoven with con-ductive yarns. When voltage is applied, the yarns warm up and generate different colors. Fabcell, 2006. Development: Dr. Akira Wakita, Keio Univer-sity, Fujisawa.

be adapted to different situations. The scientists are still working on minia-turizing the components so that, in the not-too-distant future, the individual fabric "pixel cells" can be intercon-nected and controlled via software. It will then be possible to upload images onto fabric surfaces and items of cloth-ing.[57]

Going one step further towards the de-piction of images on flexible or three-dimensional surfaces, a new camou-flaging material can be used to make people or objects invisible. Like some-thing out of a fairytale, this incredible-sounding innovation was developed at the University of Tokyo. The camou-flaging material or piece of clothing is covered in a **retroreflective layer** that consists of countless glass micro-beads. This "magic fabric" reflects the light back at the exact same angle that it arrived. A dynamic system of video cameras and projectors works togeth-er, first to record the scene concealed by the object and then to project this image data onto the object itself. The viewer is equipped with a special head-mounted device that analyzes the pre-cise direction of his or her vision. The information signals from the cameras are superimposed and the resulting image is projected onto the object at the correct angle and focal sharpness. The person or object covered in ret-roreflective material now appears to vanish because the viewer can see right through. With this technology, even moving objects can be made transparent without optical dis-tortion. Although still in its infancy, the technology has already been utilized to provide a moving car with a "transparent cockpit." This enables the early recognition of obstacles and road users, thereby helping to prevent traffic accidents.[59]

58 — Thermochromic surfaces represent changes in temperature with color changes. Here, the effect is used in a charming way to visualize the temperature of a radiator. The thermochromic coating responds to the heat by changing color, thereby transform-ing an everyday radiator into a decorative interior design element. It also offers a practical reminder to turn the heating down at appropriate times such as when leaving the apartment. Thermochromic Wallpaper. Design: Elisa Strozyk, Berlin.

59 — A retroreflective surface acts as "camouflage material." Using a special head-mounted device with an integrated system of video cameras and projectors, it is possible to make objects or people appear transparent.

Responsive – Color-changing

60 — Photoreactive surface that reacts to UV light and changes color
from transparent to varying shades of blue depending on the intensity
of the sunlight. OR, 2008. Design: Orproject, London.

Responsive – Color-changing

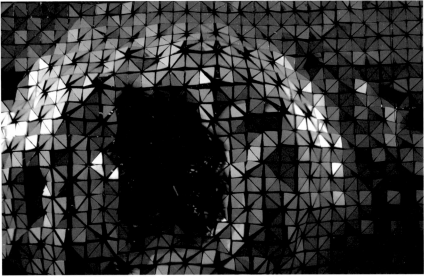

61 — The interactive surface responds in real time to various external stimuli such as sound and movement. It is controlled by a pneumatic system that generates changing images and reliefs on the surface at high speed.
Hyposurface. Design & development: Hyposurface Corp., Prof. Mark Goulthorpe, Cambridge.

D — 3.3   **Responsive** – Shape-changing

3.3 Shape-changing

Apart from their color, objects can also change their shape in response to specific external stimuli. The piezoelectric materials already mentioned for their energy-generating properties can produce voltage from a deformation process. In the reverse process, they can change their shape when voltage is applied. Another important technology in this field is **shape memory materials**. These are mostly based on a nickel titanium alloy **(nitinol)** but certain plastics are also formable according to this principle.

Shape memory alloys change between two different shapes if their temperature changes or if voltage is applied. The critical temperature can be modified for each individual project. The material is extremely resistant to corrosion and fatigue. It is capable of reversing considerable changes in shape in relation to the temperature. The technology can be used for specifically changing the length of objects or for activating small moving elements, e.g. in façades **(cf. Pixel Skin, p.128)**. Nitinol can be utilized to produce "flowing" movements, which is why engineers like to deploy it as an "artificial muscle" in robot construction. The vibration behavior of a material can also be influenced with nitinol. Nitinol rods are embedded in bridge structures and voltage is applied to them when necessary to cause a shift in the resonant frequency. This can prevent the occurrence of dangerous resonant vibrations that in extreme cases can cause bridges to collapse. Right from the outset, the development of the alloy was targeted towards influencing the vibration behavior of objects. In the 1960s, it was produced as controllable sound insulation material for submarines and battleships in order to prevent sonar detection via acoustic vibrations. Shape memory alloys have thus developed an astonishingly broad spectrum of applications from bridge safety and robot control to textile design.

The Dutch designer Mariëlle Leenders has developed Moving Textiles. Nitinol wires woven into a fabric cause the textile to contract or expand. Other than applications for clothing, the technology can also be used for sun-protection curtains that automatically unfurl when exposed to warm sunlight and roll back up when the temperature drops.[62]

62 — A fabric that can shrink or expand as required has been developed by the Dutch designer Mariëlle Leenders. She weaves fine nitinol wires into a textile. Nitinol is a shape memory alloy that changes its dimensions when voltage is applied. Movement can thus be controlled via the material's inherent properties to create products such as self-rolling sunblinds or privacy screens.
Moving Textiles. Design: Mariëlle Leenders, Eindhoven.

63 — When switched off, the lamp hangs limply from the wall. But when turned on, the lamp stiffens up and assumes a twisted shape. This is possible due to the shape memory alloys embedded in the lamp stem.
V/a.g.r.a. Animated Lamp. Design: Romolo Stanco, Piacenza.

The Responsive Surface Structure project that was developed by Steffen Reichert at Prof. Achim Menges' department at the Offenbach Academy of Art and Design aims to develop a surface capable of reacting to humidity with changes in shape. The surface changes its porosity in response to the degree of relative humidity. This occurs without employing any complicated electromechanical control devices—the process is based entirely on the structure of the natural wood material that expands when exposed to moisture. Wood fiber can hold a certain amount of bound water in relation to the relative humidity level of the surrounding atmosphere. As the saturation level rises, the wood fiber increasingly swells. But it does this in one direction only—perpendicular to its fiber direction. The **hygroscopic properties** of wood are instrumentalized here to provide a climate sensor, actuator, and regulating element in one simple component. The surface consists of a substructure upon which pairs of triangular **veneer** elements are attached parallel to their fiber direction. Because the elements change shape perpendicular to their fiber direction, the surface begins to open up as the relative humidity increases. The movement is reversible and the response time of the wood is less than 20 seconds given a substantial increase in relative humidity.

This principle enables a façade to respond locally to ventilation requirements by becoming temporarily porous. Using a parametric computational model, the individual components of the curved surface are precisely calculated and cut out of sheet material with regard to their fiber direction.[64]

The Hyposurface interactive display system functions in conjunction with a complex computerized control system. The form-generating digital input can be supplied by motion sensors or any other kind of data—from stock market figures to streams of visitors.

The standard size of the screen is 10 x 4 m. It consists of 560 actuators that serve as individually controllable pixels. This resolution allows the depiction of images and text which are dynamically rendered at speeds of up to 60 mph (approx. 95 km/h). The surface display is generated via a pneumatic system of pistons that enables these extremely fast and powerful movements. Visitors can also control the surface themselves, communicating intuitively with the wall, which then responds to their acoustic and motion input. The way the whole system moves has something living and organic that physically attracts and captivates people. "If you dance at the wall, the wall dances back at you."[61]

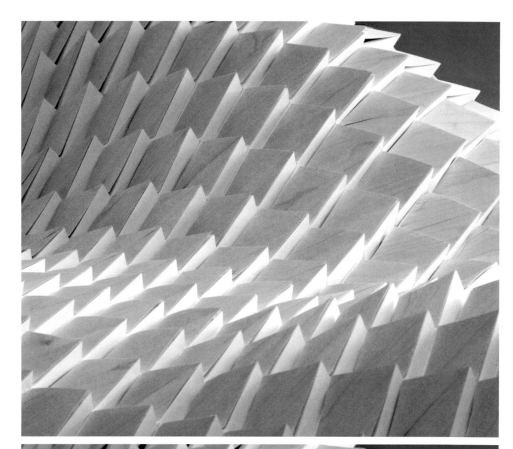

64—The veneer surface utilizes wood's characteristic of responding to increasing relative humidity by expanding in a perpendicular direction to its fiber alignment. As the relative humidity rises, the wooden "scales" attached in line with their fiber direction open and form a porous surface. This system could be used as a façade element for ventilation purposes. The reversible shape change results purely from the properties inherent within the material—no input of external energy takes place. The veneer skin changes from a closed to an open state in a matter of seconds.
Responsive Surface Structure, 2008. Offenbach Academy of Art and Design, Department of Form Generation and Materialization, Prof. Achim Menges, Steffen Reichert.

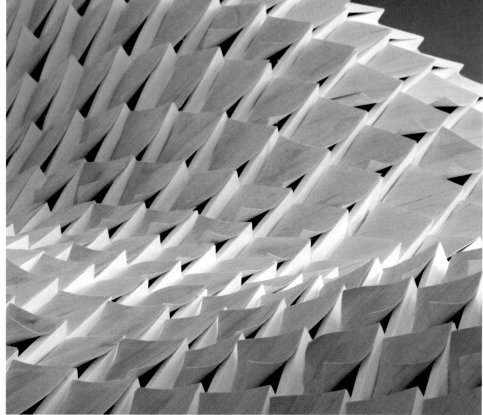

Responsive – Shape-changing

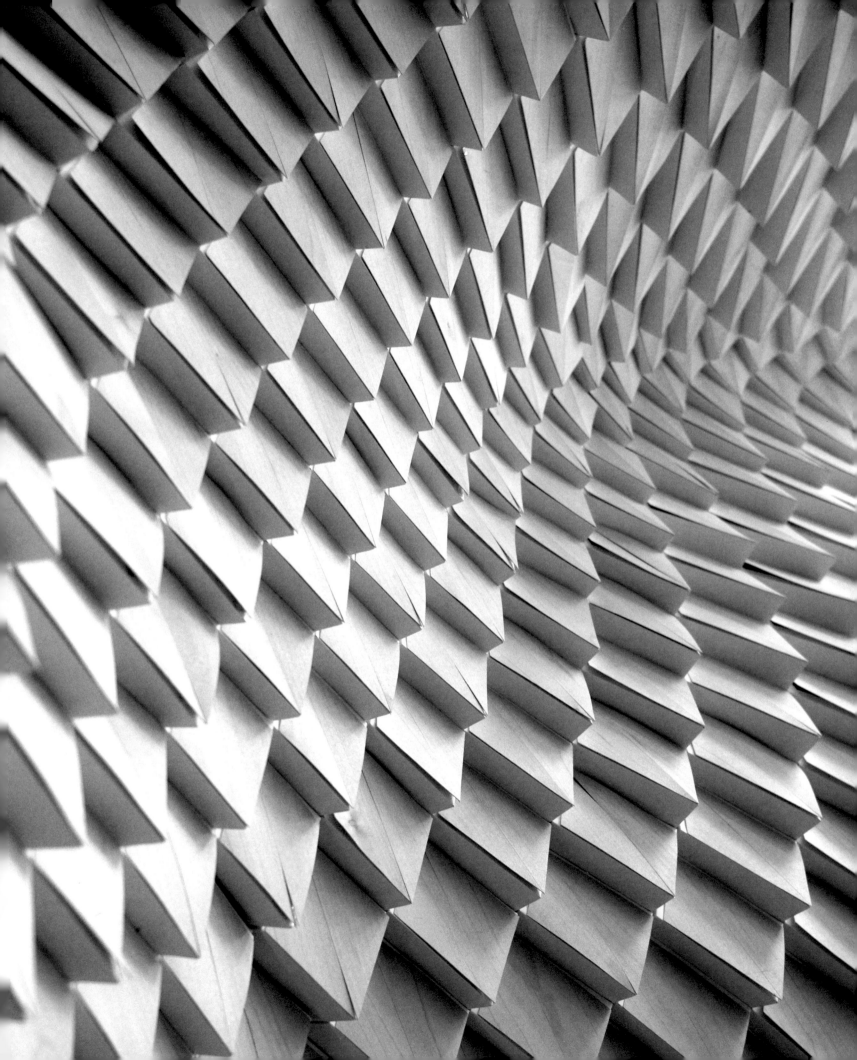

Glossary

Photovoltaics

Photovoltaic elements convert light into electrical energy. The solar cells consist of semiconducting materials that generate direct current upon exposure to light. Photovoltaic modules operate with no noise, zero emissions, and an expected lifespan of 20–30 years. Their effectiveness depends on their conversion efficiency, which expresses how much of the absorbed energy is converted into electricity in percentage terms.

A distinction is made between crystalline cells and thin-film modules that differ not just in their appearance but also in their manufacturing process and conversion efficiency.

Crystalline solar modules

The majority of solar modules in current service are the crystalline cell type. Most are cut from blocks of high-purity silicon into wafer-thin layers of approx. 0.2 mm thickness. Polycrystalline cells exhibit a clearly visible cellular structure. To enhance their capacity for absorbing sunlight, the surfaces are given an anti-reflective treatment. The color of the crystalline modules depends on the thickness of this anti-reflective coating. The individual solar cells are connected in series to form modules that have one positive and one negative terminal each. Their conversion efficiency ranges from around 14% to 20%.

Thin-film modules

Thin-film modules have been developed since the 1990s as an alternative to crystalline technology. They consist of amorphous silicon (a-Si), copper indium diselenide (CIS), copper indium gallium diselenide (CIGS), or cadmium telluride (CdTe). The coating thickness is measured in terms of microns. Two different automated processes exist for the production of thin-film modules. The first is the continuous process used to deposit photovoltaic materials onto rigid substrates such as glass. The second is the roll-to-roll method, which enables flexible substrates such as metal or plastic to be coated. Thin-film modules also perform relatively well in diffuse lighting conditions. Their surface appears dark, almost black, with a subtle trace of color that varies between bluish, greenish, and reddish depending on the manufacturing process. Their conversion efficiency ranges from 4% to 12% depending on the specific material composition.

New developments are organic solar cells and dye solar cells that can be produced at low cost using even less material. Here, sunlight is converted into voltage using either a nanocomposite of semiconducting material or an organic dye. Conversion efficiency is still low at present (around 3% for organic PV cells and between 8% and 10% for dye solar cells) and efficient lifespans still have to be developed. The technology works extremely well under weak lighting conditions such as indoor settings.
—**page 157**

Smart Materials

The term "smart materials" is generally used to describe materials that respond autonomously and immediately to their environment. If the field is restricted to materials relevant for architectural applications, the following are the most important:

Energetic materials
Photoelectric materials generate electricity upon exposure

to sunlight. Solar cells are based on the photovoltaic effect of semi-conducting materials (mostly silicon).

Piezoelectric materials generate electricity when pressure or tension is applied. The most important groups of materials are piezoelectric ceramics and polymers.

Energy-absorbing and releasing materials (phase change materials) absorb thermal energy from the surroundings when the temperature rises, and release it at a later time when the temperature drops. Their physical state changes between solid and liquid during this process.

Light-emitting materials

Photoluminescent materials are excited to emit light upon exposure to light. A distinction is made between the immediate effect of fluorescence and the long afterglowing effect of phosphorescence.

Electroluminescent materials emit light when voltage is applied. LEDs, OLEDs, and electroluminescent films are based on this principle. They emit a cold light and are extremely durable and robust.

Color-changing materials

Photochromic materials change their color upon exposure to light.

Thermochromic materials change their color in response to changes in temperature. The change is either between two different colors or from colored to colorless.

Electrochromic materials change color when voltage is applied. Electro-optical materials change their light transmissivity between transparent and opaque.

Shape-changing materials

Piezoelectric materials are induced to contract or expand when voltage is applied.

Shape memory materials change their shape when voltage is applied or when a change in temperature occurs. Possible materials include special metal alloys (nitinol) and plastics.

—page 176

E
190 – 229

Re-Material-ization

1 — Rhyolite Bottle House, 1926. The house was constructed from beer bottles during the American gold rush in Nevada in the early 20th century. The raw material was sourced from the 50 or so bars in town.

0.0 Second Life

The rapid growth of technology, population, and consumption has led to an ever-increasing exploitation of our planet's raw material resources, and our environment is not going to recover in the foreseeable future. Only recently has a new responsibility in managing the available resources begun to establish itself. This makes it all the more urgent to recognize the possibilities that sustainable materials can offer the construction industry—and to implement those insights in future buildings.

One of these strategies is the repeated use of materials or products in the form of cycles. This is not a new invention. Traditional, regional building methods have always been characterized by their efficient handling of the available resources. After demolishing a building, valuable raw materials such as wood and bricks were reclaimed and reprocessed. But due to the globalization of the modern construction industry and the complexity of building layers with integrated construction, building services, insulation, and waterproofing, this is no longer a viable option.

There are two fundamentally different types of cycle. One is based on direct utilization: **re-use**. This involves the redeployment of entire components that largely retain their original form but are often given a new purpose. The other is based on reprocessing: **re-cycling**. Here, the homogeneity of the primary material is critical in ensuring the quality of the secondary materials. If a product loses quality over the course of a recycling loop, the process is termed **downcycling**.

Renewable or **re-growing materials** are also steadily assuming greater importance. Materials produced from plants or their constituents are currently gaining a foothold in the market. After use, they can usually be disposed of via composting, thus providing nutrients for the next generation of renewable materials—an ideal cycle. The manufacturing costs are relatively low and the amount of energy required in production is ecologically viable. In addition, most regrowing materials can be produced locally, thereby eliminating high transport costs. Plant fibers are light and durable. Their structure makes them particularly suitable for manufacturing various types of insulating materials. With certain additives, they can even be used in the fabrication of load-bearing profiles and building blocks.

So the spectrum of possibilities for new, sustainable materials is broad. The onus is now on designers to develop visionary ideas that will outline new creative approaches to the materials themselves and their architectural integration. An innovative mindset that regards industry, environment, and designers as allies rather than adversaries is the forward-thinking approach to material and resources here. The recovery of resources should not be treated as a necessary evil, nor should it be allowed to degenerate into a pure marketing instrument. Rather, it must open up practical new material strategies.

1.0 Re-cycled

Over the course of a lifetime, each person in the industrialized world produces over 50 metric tons of waste. Today, this material needs to be regarded as a new resource. The building industry remains one of the largest producers of waste material in terms of quantity. For instance, more than 50 million metric tons of construction rubble and over 5 million metric tons of building site waste are produced on average every year in Germany alone. More than 80% of this huge amount of mineral rubble is already recycled as fill material for road construction and landscaping. Of the building site waste that comprises wood, glass, plastic, plaster, metal, and insulating materials, more than half (around 3 million metric tons) still ends up in the landfill. Around one quarter is recycled and the remaining quarter can be directly reused. However, it is worth noting that the total amount of waste from the building industry has actually halved in recent years—a testament to the efficient deployment of materials and leftovers.[2]

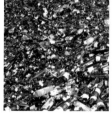

2 — Collected waste becomes the raw material for recycled products.

Numerous production processes allow used materials to be integrated into the manufacturing of new ones. For example, worldwide steel production already uses 45% scrap steel, while glass melting uses around 50% scrap glass. **Plastics**—particularly as waste from the packaging industry—represent a major part of the recycling material flow. They come in countless types with varying qualities and colors. The most suitable for recycling are thermoplastics—they can be melted down with the application of heat.

Second Life, Re-cycled

Effective material cycles are also dependent on the socio-cultural background of a given society. In developing countries, widespread poverty and shortages make it far more natural to constantly reuse materials and building products and to put them to new applications. But the manufacturing of genuinely new materials from waste products via a recycling process is frequently impossible due to deficient infrastructure and the lack of appropriate machinery.[3]

4 — Light installation made of plastic scrap that, sorted by color, illuminated a disused subway tunnel.
Farben des Konsums, 2002, Berlin. Concept: Bär und Knell, Bad Wimpfen.

3 — In India, around half the urban population live in informal settlements that evolve as independent entities within a city. The housing is built by the inhabitants themselves—the necessary materials usually consist of salvaged waste materials such as sheet metal and sacks. There is an established economic network within the settlement structures for collecting, reutilizing, and selling these scrap materials. However, the large amount of plastic waste now produced is generally unsuitable for direct reuse because plastic waste is often ripped or worn down. During the research project "Recycling Building Materials for a Sustainable Environment in India," the Institute of Building Structures and Structural Design (ITKE) at the University of Stuttgart examined how plastic waste within the existing salvage system could be recycled by hand by small local companies. Using a simple process, cement or rice sacks made from the thermoplastic material <u>polypropylene</u> (PP) can be defibrated and melted down in a press at around 200°C. This enables opaque panels to be fabricated that can then be crafted into traditional window grilles, for example. Any resulting scraps can again be melted down. Sandwich panels with a corrugated cardboard core and waterproof PP facing are another possible product—these are a major advantage during the downpours of the Indian monsoon. Hemp and jute fibers can also be added to stiffen the polypropylene and increase its bearing capacity.
New Building Materials from Recycled Waste in India. Research & development: Institute of Building Structures and Structural Design (ITKE) at the University of Stuttgart, Prof. Jan Knippers.

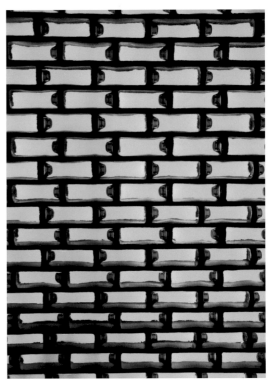

5 — The ubiquitous beer bottle can be designed to serve a new purpose in a second lifecycle. While visiting Latin America and Africa, Alfred Heineken—owner of the Heineken company—discovered that his glass beer bottles were landing in piles of garbage instead of being refilled. So in 1963 he commissioned the Dutch architect John Habraken to design a bottle that could be repurposed as a brick. The rectangular WOBO (WOrld BOttle) can be cemented with mortar and built up to form stable walls. Unfortunately, Heineken was unable to convince his marketing people of the idea's revolutionary potential—they suggested getting Marilyn Monroe to live in a WOBO House as an endorsement. The 60,000 manufactured bottles were never actually utilized for building purposes. The only existing structure is a single wall in the Heineken Museum in Amsterdam.
WOBO Bottle. Design: Prof. N.J. Habraken, Apeldoorn.

Recycling concepts

Recycling is the repeated utilization of materials or products. Recycled materials already play a major role in the building industry. From structural elements to surfaces, recycled secondary materials now provide an alternative to the primary products. Profiles made from recycled plastic, flooring made from car tires, and garden furniture made from recycled beverage bottles are just a few examples.

From an economic standpoint, market-oriented recycling loops with persistently low reprocessing costs make good sense. This type of partial reuse aims to keep products within the economic system for as long as possible. The product goes through several lifecycles but its quality deteriorates with each new cycle. This is referred to as **downcycling**, leading inexorably to the landfill after various cycles.

The goal of sustainable waste management is to create "closed-loop cycles." This idea is the basis for the **"cradle-to-cradle"** principle developed by architect William McDonough and chemist Michael Braungart. Cradle-to-cradle thinking wants to upgrade the quality of "waste" so that it is regarded as a new raw material. The concept is deeply rooted within market economics. The objective is to produce not less waste but more because the high-quality residual materials become a source for new products. Developing a secondary material is thus inherently linked to evolving the primary material. No cycle can be considered in isolation. The potential for recycling and the ensuing technology must be taken into account when first developing a primary product. This means that not only should materials be devised to ensure high quality in their recycled state, but they should also be designed to assume entirely new properties that make them suitable for a specific new purpose.

One fundamental prerequisite for recycling is the ability to break down building elements or even whole buildings into individual materials or recyclable components. A building consists of several layers that perform different tasks—envelope, structure, equipment, partitions, and furnishings. The separation of these different layers makes it possible to replace or recycle isolated components as and when required (renewal, repair). In turn, the layer itself should be made from a homogenous "monomaterial" and not assembled out of inextricably connected individual elements.

A recycling case-study house was developed by the architect Sarah Wigglesworth in London. Recycled materials are implemented here according to their specific functions and lifespans. Thus, the textile deployed as an outer skin follows the principle that individual layers of the façade must be replaceable according to their dif-

fering lifecycles. The fabric was chosen for its ideal balance between its lifespan and its "gray energy." Gray energy is the energy required to manufacture, transport, and dispose of a product. Although it may initially seem odd to deploy a material that is not particularly durable for the outermost shell, it can be replaced at the end of its lifespan with an equally low-cost and energy-efficient material.

1.1 Insulation materials

Apart from serving as visible façade layers, recycled materials can also be used as insulation within wall or floor structures. Shredded, defibrated, or granulated raw materials can easily be reprocessed into fill material or matting.

Foam **glass granulate** is a lightweight construction material with exceptional thermal and acoustic insulation properties. It is also solvent free, fireproof, and weatherproof. The material is entirely produced from recycled glass which is first ground down into a powder and then heated up with a natural foaming agent and expanded.

It can be deployed as capillary-breaking, frostproof, and pressure-resistant perimeter insulation beneath concrete ground slabs, but it is also suitable for many other insulation applications. Furthermore, energy is saved on transport because the foam glass is up to 20 times lighter than conventional gravel.[6]

Recycled cork is reclaimed from waste generated during the fabrication of cork panels or from collected bottle corks. In granulate

form it is suitable for acoustic and thermal insulation beneath flooring or screeding. With a blowing system, it can be used to backfill roof constructions or walling systems and its thermal conductivity coefficient is around 0.040 W/mK.[7]

6 — Granulated foam glass made from recycled glass is a light and highly pressure-resistant insulating material.

7 — Recycled cork granulate.

Denim scraps left over from the textile industry are now also being repurposed as insulation. The jeans material can be utilized as thermal and acoustic insulation. Its cotton fibers are treated with an ecologically safe borate solution that repels insects and mildew and has a fire-retardant effect. Borates contain bound water of crystallization that is released in the event of fire and serves to protect the fibers. Architect Renzo Piano used the recycled materi-

8 — Case-study house that accommodates office and living space. Sustainable materials were instrumental in shaping the design: The walls consist of insulating strawbales or recycled concrete sourced from local demolition yards that is filled into gabion cages. The concrete rubble inside the metal cages was designed to be load-bearing and was structurally analyzed as such. But the relevant authorities refused to grant permission for this unprecedented construction and demanded additional supporting columns. Because the building is situated close to a railway line, a high-mass wall was necessary to provide one part of the building with acoustic protection. In order to find a simple and efficient solution, sandbags were filled with a hydraulic lime-cement-sand mix and stacked up. The cloth decays with time, providing a low-tech solution for an organically shaped mass concrete wall.

9 Stock Orchard Street, London, 2004. Architecture: Sarah Wigglesworth Architects, London.

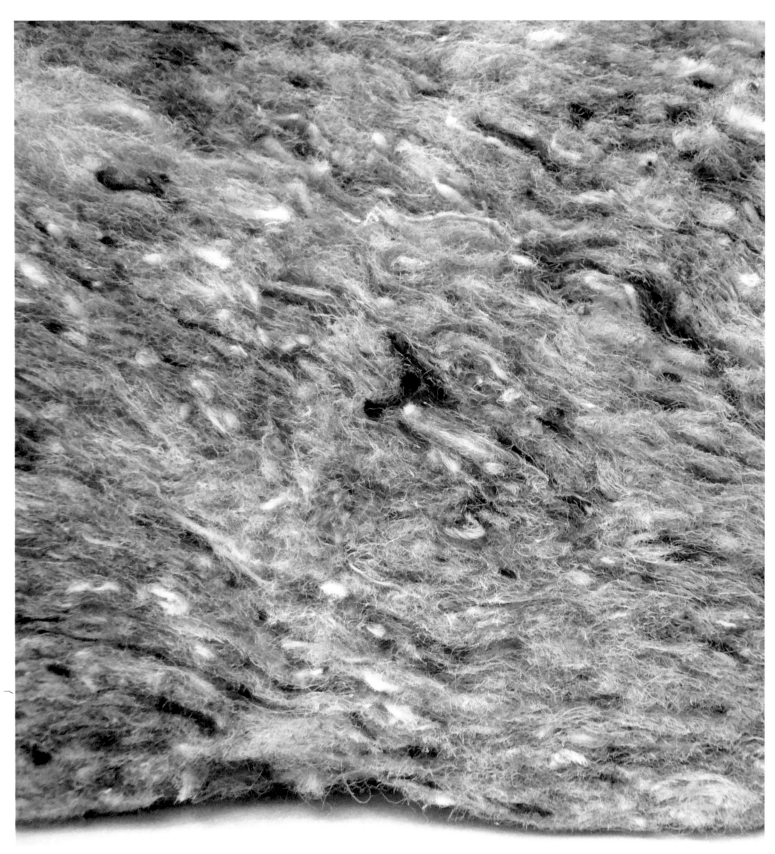

9 — Cotton insulation made of defibrated denim.

10 — For renovation projects, cellulose insulation made of recycled newspaper can be blown into roof cavities as loose flakes. The material is also available in the form of mats for wall insulation.

al in his recently completed building for the California Academy of Sciences in San Francisco—a large proportion of the building was insulated with recycled denim.[9]

Apart from cotton, the vegetable raw material **cellulose** is also suitable for insulation. Cellulose is the base material in the manufacturing of paper and can thus also be recovered from used paper products. In order to fabricate cellulose insulation material, **newspapers** are broken down into a coarsely fibrous pulp, once again mixed with boric salt and then processed into flakes. Recycled newspaper can be deployed to particularly good effect in the renovation of existing buildings. The material is blown via a tube into the wall structure on site, whereupon it condenses to form a wind-tight and seamless thermal skin. This is especially practical with inaccessible areas such as low attics and cavity floors. The material can be returned to the manufacturer for disposal and recycled again. Its thermal conductivity coefficient is 0.040 W/mK. Recently, cellulose insulation made from newspaper has also become available in the form of matting. Thanks to its high density, the matting also provides outstanding acoustic protection.[10]

1.2 Structural materials

Recycled cellulosic paper labels have even be used as construction material by the Japanese architect Shigeru Ban. This remarkable project arose in collaboration with the Finnish company UPM, which manufactures wood products and printing papers. Large quantities of residue material are generated every day in the production of its laminated self-adhesive paper labels.

The high-quality paper-plastic mixture consists of 60% **cellulose fiber** and 40% **polypropylene** (part of which is itself recycled). The plastic component gives the material its mechanical strength and humidity resistance. Even for outdoor applications, no additional surface treatment is required. The material is virtually free of lignin—the polymeric binding agent in wood that has a tendency to gray. Thus it exhibits good resistance to fading when exposed to UV radiation. The material can be used in extrusion and injection molding processes. The architect's collaboration with industry gave rise to a floor covering, a furniture system, and an entire pavilion. All these products make use of the material's

specific characteristics. Design meets recycled material—a rare combination that is all the more interesting as a result.[12-16]

For the construction of the pavilion, Shigeru Ban used a preexisting semifinished product: the company already recycles the surplus material left over from the production of self-adhesive labels for its own use, extruding them into L profiles that are deployed to protect the edges of packaged paper stacks.[16]

The architect used these profiles to construct a 40 meter long pavilion for the Finnish furniture manufacturer Artek. First

11 — PET plastic beverage bottles are ideal for recycling and can be reprocessed into polyester fiber for the textile industry, for example. Five water bottles provide enough material for a T-shirt. A chair is made by processing PET felt mats. The polymer fiber is thermopressed into shape in a single step. No further additives are necessary. The result is a piece of furniture made of a monomaterial that can easily be recycled again after use. The surface has good acoustic properties and is easy to clean. The light and stackable chair is reminiscent of a drape that continues to hold its position after the chair underneath has gone, like a soft piece of fabric standing on its own. Nobody Chair for HAY, Denmark, 2007. Design: Komplot, Copenhagen.

he had the material tested for its structural properties. It turned out to be a relatively soft composite—not a structurally strong material. But this was exactly what Ban found challenging.

As he explained in describing his design approach: "Material doesn't need to be strong to be a strong structure." The load-bearing structure was thus designed in accordance with the given properties of the profiles. The L shapes were partly combined to form T or X-shaped cross sections with greater structural stability. These make up the structural frame of the pavilion. All the joints are held together with releasable connections to make the building easy to assemble and dismantle. Even the exterior surfaces of the pavilion are clad with the L profiles, which are arranged in an interlocking pattern to form a waterproof skin. Thus, one and the same profile is combined in different ways to suit varying purposes—from the structural components to the façade and the roof.

The floor of the building is also made of recycled profiles that were extruded from the residual material of self-adhesive labels.

This approach demonstrates an innovative way of working with recycled products. The material is reinterpreted and its role is opened up to encompass a new application. But vision is required on the part of the designers to materialize an idea as radical as the "soft construction" concept.

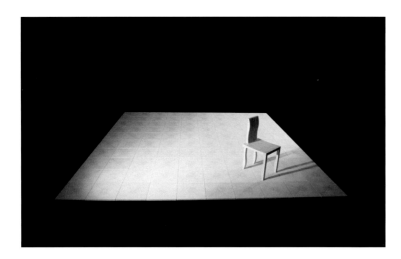

12 — Floor and wall covering system made of a cellulose-plastic composite. Each tile acquires a unique marbled surface in the recycling process and exudes a subtle vibrancy within the overall surface. In addition, the smooth texture and monochrome color of the tiles render them high-quality in character. The modules are clipped together to form large surfaces. Electrical wiring can be run through the cavity on the back of the tile. ProFi Floor, UPM, 2009. Design: Shigeru Ban, Tokyo/Paris.

13 — The 10-Unit System is a modular furniture system. The structural and formal basis of this system is a single L-shaped component that can be combined in different positions. In a few simple moves, the components can be assembled to form a table, bench or chair. 10-Unit System, Artek, 2009. Design: Shigeru Ban, Tokyo/Paris.

Re-cycled – Structural materials

15 — The paper-plastic composite that accumulates as scrap material in the production of self-adhesive labels has been utilized as the base material for semifinished profiles, building products, furniture, and even a temporary pavilion.

14 — The pavilion was designed for and presented at the Milan Furniture Fair 2007. Its structural elements, façade, and roof were all made from an existing recycled profile that was deployed in various combinations to suit specific purposes. The structurally weak L shapes were bolted together to form T cross sections with greater bearing capacity, which were then joined to construct 21 truss framework modules. These form the core load-bearing structure of the pavilion. The entire construction is stiffened with steel tension cables fitted in every second roof and wall bay. Components in the structural framework that are exposed to particular strain carry an increased risk of buckling. The T profiles were doubled up here and strengthened into X-shaped cross sections consisting of four L profiles bundled together. The roof and walls of the pavilion are clad with yet another geometric variation of the base material. Here the Ls were arranged in an interlocking pattern and stuck together to produce large waterproof panels with a zigzag cross section. These panels could be prefabricated in the factory.
Artek Pavilion, Milan, 2007. Architecture: Shigeru Ban Architects, Tokyo/Paris.
— page 202/203

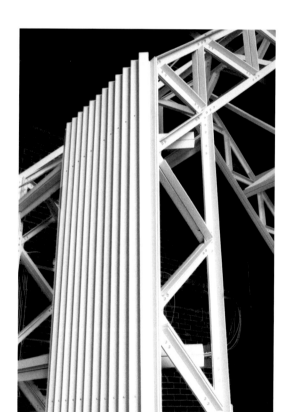

16 — L profiles that serve as edge protectors for stacks of paper were utilized by Shigeru Ban as the basic module for the pavilion structure.

14 — Artek Pavilion, Milan, 2007. Architecture: Shigeru Ban Architects, Tokyo/Paris.
— page 201

Re-cycled – Structural materials

1.3 Finish Materials

Beyond structural applications, recycled materials are now also breaking into new territory with their visual characteristics.

For example, the technical resilience of **glass** is not its only interesting attribute. As a recycled product, it reveals a unique and engaging aesthetic. The material is highly suited to being fed into a second lifecycle as panels, tiles, or mosaics through the melting down of production leftovers.

Window glass can be recycled, crushed, and then compressed at high temperature and pressure into solid panels to pro-

17 — Panel made of recycled window glass.

duce a material of considerable aesthetic appeal and outstanding structural hardness. With backlighting, it almost seems like a sheet of ice and gains a somewhat mystical aura. Due to its recycled structure, this secondary material acquires a unique new identity that is completely independent of the primary product.[17]

Likewise, bottles from waste glass collection can also be reprocessed into new high-quality materials for interior finishes. The color mixtures are diverse and can be customized to suit client requirements. The glass fragments are bonded together with a solvent-free resin and cast into panels via a "cold" energy-saving process. Finally, the surface is smoothly polished.[18]

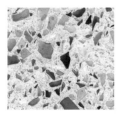

18 — Glass scraps sorted according to color give rise to a decorative and durable surface that is particularly suitable for heavy-duty kitchen surfaces.

Various polymers—the group of **thermoplastics**—can be recycled by melting. For industrial reprocessing, the materials are first granulated and then cast into molded forms or extruded into profiles.

The range of recycled plastic materials has grown relatively broad. The color and texture can be customized to influence the appearance and feel of the plastic surface. Leaving the "confetti" aesthetic behind, the simple fact that the material shows evidence of a previous life can be an interesting trait in itself. The primary material is key here in determining the color, pattern, strength, and texture of the recycled material, which allows a certain degree of customization. Even discarded commodities and rejects from industrial production can be processed into panel material.[24-26]

— **"Plastic recycling" page 228**

In a panel material that gives some indication of its origins as tetrapack beverage cartons, colored particles of packaging are discernable alongside tiny segments of aluminum from the original inner coating. This glistening effect is what gives the material its special character. The cartons are first chopped up into particles of about 5 mm in diameter and precompressed. The material is then compacted in a heating press, whereupon the **polyethylene component** of the beverage carton melts. This gives the panel its subsequent stability and moisture resistance without requiring any further additives. The material can then be processed to requirements and finished with various surfaces via laminating, veneering, or lacquering.[21]

It is even possible to manufacture high-quality abrasion-proof floor surfaces from recycled car tires. The tires are shredded into granulate and a **polyurethane** binding agent is added. The color can be modified by the addition of synthetic **rubber granules**. The

19 — Car tires are turned into a vibration-dampening floor surface.

elastic surface dampens structure-borne sound and is slip proof, abrasion resistant, and easy to clean. Sheets of the material are simple to lay in loose or glued form, making them ideal for tasks with short set-up times such as trade fair construction. After use, the material can again be recycled.[19]

New EU directives on the recyclability of electronic products are presenting the recycling industry with new challenges. For example, around 45 million cell phones are currently in use in the United Kingdom alone. Fifteen million of these are replaced each year with new devices. Most of the huge quantity of discarded cell phones is shredded and used as fill material in road building and other civil engineering applications. But this waste can also be upgraded into a new material by pressing it into panels. This is done with just heat and pressure—no additives or binding agents are necessary. The primary products are processed in large presses at 180°C. The individual shells with their unique features—stickers and the occasional scratched-in number—remain clearly discernable. This individuality makes each panel a one-off and gives the material its distinct identity. The 120 x 180 cm panels are suitable for interior application.[25]

One further type of recycled product is the "wellie" panel. Here, the base material comes from children's rubber boots. Children rapidly grow out of their footwear and old shoes tend to get thrown out with the household garbage. But in this case, boots are collected in pairs and compacted into soft panels that can be utilized as elastic surfaces for furniture or seating. [26]

20 — The redevelopment of the lively square at the heart of Newcastle demanded a design and materials hard-wearing enough to cope with considerable foot traffic both day and night. The surface also needed to offer strength and durability for emergency vehicle access. Sustainable tiles were designed specifically for the project using shards of recycled blue bottles set in a white resin. The resin provides a practical and strong material for the design, whilst the glass guarantees color in years to come. The tiles were set in rows and edged with brass strips. At certain places the surface is peeled back to form benches, revealing glazed voids which provide space for local artists to exhibit their work to the public.
Blue carpet, Newcastle, 2002. Design: Heatherwick Studio, London.

21 — Panel material made from recycled beverage cartons. No adhesives are added during reprocessing. The thermoplastic ingredient in the material melts to provide the new panel with its strength.

22 — High-pressure decorative laminate with texture. The surface of this mass product has a unique feel. The embedded fibers are reclaimed from recycled coffee and vegetable sacks and then scattered into the surface.

Actively emphasizing the visual character of recycled material is a new approach within the materials industry. Until recently, recycled products were rarely promoted on the basis of their appearance. Material manufacturers are often unaware of the design potential and marketability of their products. Product promotion tends to focus on technical properties and ecological aspects, while the actual surface is regarded as somehow inferior and concealed beneath lacquering or laminates.

The advantage with recycled materials made from used products is that each panel is totally unique. The client can stipulate the individual combination of materials and granulates to be reprocessed, thereby influencing the surface outcome during the production process. Visible evidence of the primary material actually enhances the semantic value of a product. Knowing that a material is made from recycled coat hangers, rubber boots, banknotes, or cell phone shells gives it a unique history. Some unusual raw materials are only available in limited quantities. This shortage could be leveraged as a positive marketing instrument in the sense of a limited edition.

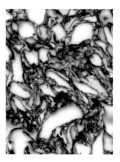  

24 — Coarsely broken down and recycled food packaging is mixed with yellow plastic pipes and fused together to form a kind of pop marble pattern.

25 — Panel material made of cell phone shells melted under pressure and heat.

26 — Children's rubber boots are compacted into soft mats.

So instead of implying some kind of drawback, recycling takes on an added value that can even provide a competitive edge over conventional products. In this sense, recycling needs to be viewed as an upgrade. The goal is not to provide imitations of primary products but to create secondary materials with unique identities and new properties.

23 — The polyester material consists of recycled plastic and is itself 100% recyclable. The resilient surface can even be used for high-quality bathroom furnishings. Joints can be smoothed down almost to the point of invisibility.

2.0 Re-used

Consumer society keeps producing ever more things of which an excess is already available. But instead of adding still more new commodities, existing ones could be used in new ways. Products can be directly reused without having to recycle their constituent materials. Reuse is the term for a redeployment that also frequently involves a reinterpretation of the material's original function. In contexts where raw materials are in short supply or poverty is widespread, this principle is an everyday reality due to the lack of alternatives. Waste products acquire a new value from being reused. For instance, car tires can be repurposed as seating, and bottles can serve as building material.

In the context of the industrialized world, large quantities of materials and products are left untouched in stockpiles or stem from overproduction and often end up being scrapped. This represents another new field of activity for designers and architects. In the case of reuse, designers do not focus on some precisely defined end result that can only be realized with precisely defined materials. Rather, they adapt as far as possible whatever materials are currently available. The resulting design solutions may not be entirely perfect but this is their charm. There is a surprising and irrational aspect about reused *objets trouvés* that were clearly not purpose-built for their new application.

The website Superuse showcases examples in which designers and architects have reused material along these lines. It also serves as an information resource—sharing knowledge on what particular industrial products or leftover materials are currently available and where. "Harvest maps" can filter available material sources in terms of their proximity to a particular location. This helps to avoid inefficient transport routing. Logistics and communication management thus become key tools in the reuse of materials. With its database structure, the Superuse principle can also work on larger scales and is not restricted to individual projects.

The founders of this platform—2012Architecten from Rotterdam—are committed to the "material designs space" concept in their own construction projects. For example, car windshields are

28 — High-quality leftovers from the <u>leather</u> industry, usually disposed of as waste, can be punched to small, clover-like forms, which can be combined to form a carpet without gluing or sewing. The modular design makes it possible for the owner of the carpet to repeatedly change or expand its form as desired and to combine different colors.
"Feliz". Design: Manon Juliette, Amsterdam.

27 — With just three weeks to complete the project, this light installation was built for the Milan Furniture Fair 2009 from 702 plastic one-gallon containers that are reinterpreted here as light objects. Thus an everyday plastic commodity is repurposed as a brick within a 5 x 8 meter surface. The backlighting gives the installation a powerful presence.
RE/DO Light Installation, Milan, 2009. Design: PSLAB Beirut.

29 — This modular mobile space station was build from disused washing machines as an experiment to design architecture from waste in 2003. It has been traveling Holland since then, functioning as cafe, restaurant, office, and shop and was finally installed as an espresso bar in the faculty of architecture in Delft. Unfortunately it then burned down with the building in the big fire in 2008.
Miele Space Station at the Parkfeest-Festival, Venlo, 2006. Architecture: 2012Architecten, Rotterdam.

30 — 72,000 used carpet tiles are held in place
and compressed by a construction involving a
wooden ring beam and hidden metal posts.
The tiles form the weatherproof exterior wall
of this low-cost housing project.
Lucy's House, Alabama, 2002. Architecture:
Rural Studio, Auburn.

stockpiled in large quantities, partly to cover availability for older vehicles. The result is a huge number of identical windshields in brand new condition. Being made of **safety glass**, they can be deployed for both façades and interior elements. The architects converted the material into shelving for a shoe store. 150 brand new Audi 100 windshields form two elegantly curved segments with the fitting area in the middle. Basic suction cups provide the fixings for the glass panels.[33]

The Rural Studio—part of Auburn University in the USA—develops sustainable buildings as self-construction projects with the help of students. For Lucy's House—a low-cost housing project in Alabama—they used discarded **carpet tiles** to construct an exterior wall. 72,000 of the quadratic nylon tiles are stacked in an interlocking pattern. Steel posts are hidden in the carpet wall for stabilization. These posts are screwed into a wooden ring beam that rests on top of the carpet tiles, pressing them together. The layered shell has significantly better thermal insulation properties than the wood-frame walls that are typical in the region. Both the installation and the properties of this unusual building material were tested with particular attention to water absorption and fire resistance. Although the wall does absorb water on its exterior surface, it dries out completely within a day because of the low water retention capacity of its synthetic fibers.[30]

The façade of a temporary 400 m² pavilion that was built for the 2008 Architecture Biennale in Chile is also made of reused industrial materials. It was designed as a temporary extension for an existing museum, providing an additional auditorium and exhibition space. It was the architect's intention to deploy only reused or reusable materials for the construction and interior. The basic structure is provided by scaffolding while the envelope is made from aluminum strips. The materials are production leftovers that can theoretically be recycled but in this case were directly reused, thus eliminating the additional energy input necessary for a recycling process. The translucence of the envelope results in a fascinating play of light after dark. During the day, the structure appears solid and metallic.[31]

Reuse thus offers a definite alternative to recycling because no energy is spent on breaking down or pulverizing materials and then pressing them back into new shapes. But in order to work with reusable products, architects need to rethink their creative approach to planning and detailing. Design thus becomes a re-creative process.

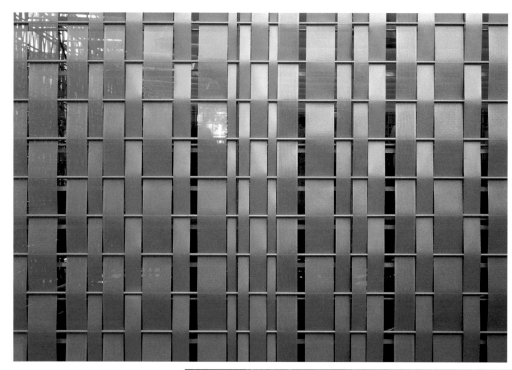

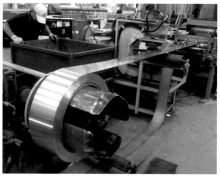

31 — The façade of the exhibition pavilion consists of perforated translucent
aluminum strips that are off-cuts from the manufacture of shading products.
The strips with widths of 10 – 30 cm are interwoven with horizontal metal struts
to create a vivid surface.
Pavilion for the XVI Chilean Architecture Biennale, Santiago de Chile, 2008.
Architecture: Felipe Assadi + Francisca Pulido Architects, Santiago de Chile.
— page 210/211

Re-used

31—Pavilion for the XVI Chilean Architecture Biennale. Santiago de Chile, 2008. Architecture: Felipe Assadi + Francisca Pulido Architects, Santiago de Chile.
—page 209

Re-used

32 — Standard pallets are a product that can be found all over the world. At the end of their life cycle, they are usually disposed of by burning. The prototype of the Palettenhaus (Pallet House) was developed as a proposal for sensible reuse. 800 refurbished pallets are required for the construction of a 60 m² pallet house (at a price of approx. €5 per pallet). The pallet is used as a modular façade, ceiling and wall element. The supporting structure, thermal insulation and installations are located between the pallets. Cellulose or sand as filling material can be used for insulation. This simple concept is interesting for emergency accommodations, for example, but it can also be upgraded to construct permanent residential buildings by applying appropriate glazing.
Palettenhaus, 2008. Architecture: SPa(r), Vienna.

33 — Although leftovers make up 90% of the interior, the manner of their deployment creates an interior design that is innovative and high quality.
Car windshields still in pristine condition after years of storage are utilized as wall shelving to display shoes in a store.
Duchi Shoe Shop, Scheveningen, 2004. Design: 2012Architecten, Rotterdam.

Re-used

3.0 Re-grown

The search for materials that fulfill the demands of sustainable production and resource saving is bearing new fruit—the materials of the future are growing on their own instead of being produced with massive energy input. The ancient tradition of plant-based building materials has now been translated into a contemporary approach that complies with current technical requirements and production methods.

Needless to say, renewable wood never lost its significance and to this day remains a ubiquitous building material—from structural elements to furniture surfaces. But in the following section, the focus will be on vegetable building materials that are taking a brand-new or long-forgotten approach in terms of their manufacturing process, material, or properties.

Apart from conventional types of wood, many plant types are now being discovered as potential new materials with attractive visual characteristics. There are now wall coverings made of **coconut shells** that are by-products from the food industry, or floor coverings and building panels made of the rapidly regrowing bamboo. Borrowing from traditional weaving and braiding techniques, modern furniture can be manufactured from plant fibers. Palm and bamboo leaves can be defibrated and processed into textiles that are not only durable but also aesthetically appealing.

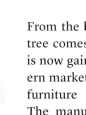

34 — Mosaic tiles made from coconut shells.

From the **bark** of the East African fig tree comes a traditional material that is now gaining a foothold in the western market as a decorative surface for furniture and automobile interiors. The manufacturing process involves stripping the bark off the tree by hand, boiling it, and then softening it up by beating it for days with wooden clappers until it is finally reduced to a flat cloth. By applying sealants to the surface, it is possible to produce abrasion-protected and water-repellent variations and even artificial leather quality. The debarked tree trunk is protected from drying out with palm leaves and can be harvested again one year later.[35, 38]

35 — One material with extremely versatile usage is bark cloth, a bast fleece from the trunk of the East African fig tree. In 2005, the centuries-old manual fabrication process for this material between wood and textile was declared a world cultural heritage by UNESCO. The surface character of this "wooden fleece" varies depending on the age of the tree, the timing of the harvest, and the working methods of the bark cloth manufacturer. The tree is kept alive in this manufacturing process—the bark regrows and can be harvested again.

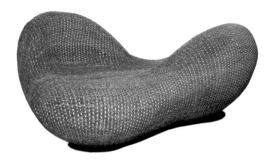

36 — One extremely robust and rapidly growing type of plant is the thick-stemmed water hyacinth. It originates from Brazil and was brought to North America, Asia, and Africa in the 19th century. It floats on water and covers large surfaces like a green mat. In the absence of natural enemies, it proliferates at extraordinary speed—doubling its surface area every two weeks. The weed deprives the water of oxygen and light. Fish and plants die out and the water silts up as a result. Harvesting and utilizing the water hyacinth as a raw material is an intelligent solution to the problem. Sushi Daybed. Design: PIE studio, New York.

37 — Straw insulation in combination with a ventilated façade. Achleitner Organic Farm, Eferding, 2004. Architecture: Architekturplus, Paul Seeber, Vahrn.

Re-grown

38 — Wall covering made of white barkcloth.
Loft, Hamburg, 2009. Architecture: Graft, Berlin.

Re-grown

39 — Washed-up seaweed is transformed from a waste product into a new raw material.

Re-grown – Renewable insulation

3.1 Renewable insulation

Plant fibers are particularly suitable for insulation purposes. The insulating effect is produced by air cells enclosed within the spaces between the fibers. Although panels made of wood fiber and wood wool have been deployed in construction for years, insulation made of flax, hemp, and seaweed has yet to break through into broader usage. The vegetable fibers exhibit consistently good insulation properties and their thermal conductivity coefficient is around 0.040 W/mK. Furthermore, they have the characteristic of being able to absorb and release moisture. This means that they contribute towards a balanced and healthy interior climate. The fibers are treated with boric salt that provides the necessary fire protection and prevents infestation by insects, rodents, and mildew. After use, the vegetable insulation materials can be disposed of via composting. Another advantage of natural insulation materials is that they can theoretically be grown in the vicinity. This is why special attention should be paid to local occurrences when selecting a suitable insulation material.
— **"Regrowing insulation materials" page 228**

Ubiquitously available grasses and **straw** were used as insulation in the very first buildings constructed by man. If straw is highly compacted, it can be deployed not just for insulation purposes but also as a load-bearing structural element. This building material is emission-free and can be used for interior construction and for load-bearing exterior walls. Compacted straw displays excellent fire resistance in fire tests. The compaction makes it behave similarly to wood—it chars on the outside, thus creating a fire barrier.[48]

40 — Spheroid granules of foamed raw algae are joined with starch into a molded component.
Development: Verpackungszentrum Graz in collaboration with the Graz Technical University, Institute for Process Engineering.

41 — Prototype of a thermal insulation panel made from purified, dried, and compacted seaweed. Development: Institute of Wood and Fiber Materials Technology, TU Dresden, Sören Tech.

42 — Grass insulation.

43 — Sea balls of matted seaweed fibers that are produced by wave movement on the ocean floor.

44 — Seaweed fibers are fire resistant by nature.

Flax and **hemp** are also outstanding natural insulation materials. Due to the presence of natural bitterns, they are inherently resistant to infestation by insects and mice. The utilized short flax fibers, hemp fibers, and shives are actually by-products of flax and hemp cultivation. Their deployment in the manufacturing of insulation materials is thus a meaningful way of processing them. Furthermore, hemp regrows very quickly.

Field grass consists of natural cellulose that is an excellent insulation material. The fibers are purified and nutrients such as proteins and natural sugars are removed, thereby eliminating the possibility of insect infestation or damage by mice. Boric salt treatment provides the necessary fire protection and prevents mildew infestation. The material can be sprayed into cavities as thermal or acoustic insulation material or deployed as fill material.[42]

The grass of the ocean—**seaweed**—is a marine plant that consists of long slender leaves. It can be found throughout the world. Severed bits of vegetation in the form of loose leaves or "sea balls" are washed up in huge quantities on the coast, where they dry out. For centuries, seaweed was traditionally used for insulation in coastal regions and the technology is now experiencing a renaissance. Washed-up seaweed is considered a nuisance in tourist areas and removed at considerable expense. This "waste" can now be recycled and converted into a high-quality building product. Due to its natural salt content, the seaweed can be processed without chemical additives. It is flame resistant, mildew resistant, and long lasting. The leaves can be processed into mats or chopped up and used as thermal insulation for roofs, ceilings, and walls with the help of conventional blowing equipment.[39, 41, 43, 44]

The utilization of sea balls for insulation purposes is a new development. Prof. Richard Meier from the Heidelberg School of Engineering and Architecture discovered that these brown spheroids

45 — Sheep wool is a natural insulation material that can absorb moisture without losing its insulating properties, thereby ensuring a balanced interior climate. It also binds air pollutants.

could make an innovative building material. The compressed fiber balls that are produced by wave movement on the ocean floor are easy to reprocess after being unraveled. The primary energy input is minimal. This innovative insulation material is currently at the testing stage.

Another new development is an algae-based foam material. **Algae** exist in huge quantities worldwide. They are an extremely fast-growing raw material. During the manufacturing process, the algae are expanded using just air. The material exhibits inherent flame-retardant properties. After use, the product can be composted or recycled along with waste paper. Although currently still being developed in a research project, the material could in the long term serve as a substitute for expanded polystyrene (EPS).[40]

Two graduates of the Rensselaer Polytechnic Institute in Troy, New York, have developed regrowing insulation materials with low production costs and the capacity to be manufactured anywhere in the world. Eben Bayer and Gavin McIntyre created a biodegradable insulation material out of fungi. The filamentous structure of the **fungus mycelia** that finely permeates its surroundings is the core component of this innovative material. For initial tests, the two inventors mixed fungus mycelia and perlite granulate with water, hydrogen peroxide, and recycled newspaper. The fungus mixture was then filled into a convenient plastic container and kept for several days in a dark and quiet spot under the bed of one of the developers. The mycelium grows in the dark, feeding on the organic substances contained within the cellulose of the newspaper. The insulating perlite pellets—expanded spheres of igneous rock—become "grown in" during this process and the expanding mass fills the exact shape of the container. Further tests followed with increasingly sophisticated techniques, gradually developing the material into a highly efficient product. Vegetable production waste from industry can also serve as nutrition for the fungi. The basic substance can be varied depending on the local circumstances. For example, leftovers can be utilized from cotton production in the United States or from rice production in Asia. These local sources of raw materials help to minimize energy and costs for transport. No oil resources are involved in the production process—the fungi do their work without light or additional warmth. In order to stop the growing process of the biomaterial, the mixture is heated once to 43°C to extract the water. The required energy for this process is taken from low-energy sources via forced convection or solar technology.

Fungus-based insulation is also setting out to challenge the conventional and widespread **EPS insulation** manufactured from petrochemicals. Its properties can definitely compete—the insulating performance is equivalent and compressive resistance is high. Furthermore, the production costs of this natural material are significantly lower than those of chemically manufactured products. The new biomaterial is currently being tested for compliance with international standards, and its worldwide market launch is imminent.[46, 47]

46 — <u>Acoustic panels</u> made of fungus insulation.

47— Fungus mycelium-based insulation material. During the growth process, the filamentous mycelium structure permeates and binds a substrate made of perlite granulate and cellulose-based nutrients. The material can "grow" in complete darkness with no energy input. The biological process is stopped by heating the mixture once.

Natural insulation materials can even be deployed for fire prevention and air improvement. As a "regrowing" insulation material with animal origins, **sheep wool** exhibits strong moisture performance that distinguishes it from plant-based insulation materials. The wool can absorb up to 30% of its own weight in moisture without changing its thermal conductivity, which is around 0.040 W/mK. But care must be taken with construction to ensure that the moisture can escape. Sheep wool also improves interior air because it consists of 97% keratin, which binds air pollutants such as formaldehyde.[45]

Corn starch can even serve as **fire protection**. Sugar extracted from corn starch is combined with ammonium polyphosphate, foaming agent, and other components and processed into a fire protection coating for wood products and solid wood. In the event of fire, the foaming agent expands to form a carbon foam layer that protects the wood underneath. The flame retardant is suitable for interior use and is completely transparent.

48 — The 25 cm thick sandwich element is both load-bearing and insulating layer in one. The highly compressed inner and outer layers (4 cm) enclose the more porous, thermally insulating core. The modular building system enables prefabrication in the factory and quick, dry installation on the construction site. The greenish shimmering weather-proofing that is applied on top of the straw elements consists of Scobalith plastic corrugated panels. With the exception of a concrete core, the entire interior was also built from straw panels.
Straw House, Eschenz, 2005. Architecture: Felix Jerusalem, Zurich.

Re-grown – Renewable insulation

3.2 Bioplastics

Looking to the future, another field emerging on the horizon is opening up new perspectives—biopolymers. Unlike petroleum-based polymers, these are made from renewable raw materials and/or are biodegradable. Biodegradable means that organic material is broken down by microbes and converted into water, CO_2, energy, and cell mass. The amount of CO_2 released is no greater than the amount previously absorbed from the atmosphere by the plants.

The most important groups of bioplastics are thermoplastic starch, cellulose acetate, and polylactic acid (PLA). The primary substances are obtained from natural materials such as potatoes (starch-based), cotton (cellulose-based), or the fermentation of sugar and starch (lactic acid-based). These pure biopolymers are also mixed with biodegradable polymers such as polyesters into **"polymer blends."** These mixtures are highly suitable for industrial processing on standard machinery.

49 — Ultralight transparent honeycomb insulation panel that is assembled from cellulose-based films and used in railcar construction.

Lactic acid-based polymers can be used to manufacture crystal-clear films—ideal for the packaging industry. Depending on the specific requirements, the thermoplastic material can be engineered to either biodegrade rapidly or retain its function for years. Once processed into film, PLA is printable and breathable, making it an excellent option for food packaging. If PLA fibers are processed into 3D fabric, they can be turned into a biodegradable geotextile that promotes plant growth.[59]

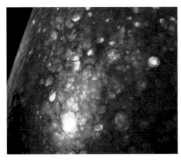

50 — Stable cellulose-based material obtained from plant fibers or old paper without the need for additional binding agents. It can be pressed into shape.

51 — Paper pulp mixed with polylactic acid (PLA) is the base material for a "paper" chair for children that is both light and robust. The innovative surface feels like paper but the durability of the material is comparable with plastic or wood due to the special composition of the material. Extensive durability tests were conducted in order to prepare the product for being used by children. The final pressing process gives the material its durability. The chair is completely eco-friendly—it can be composted and yet remains water-resistant when temporarily exposed to moisture.
Parapu Chair, 2009, Södra Pulp Labs. Design: Claesson Koivisto Rune, Stockholm.

52 — A "polymer blend" made of the bioplastic PLA (polylactic acid) and petrochemically based biodegradable polyester. The films can be processed into packaging or supermarket carrier bags that can be converted into compost along with other biowaste.

53 — Panels made of resin-bonded ground almond shells that are produced as leftovers in the food-processing industry.

54 — "Liquid wood" consists of cellulose and lignin and can be cast and processed like thermoplastic polymer.

One transparent type of thermal and acoustic insulation from the automotive industry is based on cellulose acetate. The material is biodegradable and can be recycled. It has already been used for over 60 years for insulating Scandinavian railcars. Designers have now discovered the material, not least because of its translucent visual properties.[49]

Further bioplastics can be produced on the basis of the natural polymer **lignin**. Lignin serves as a stiffening substance in the structure of wood and is the most common organic material in nature apart from cellulose. "Liquid wood" consists of lignin mixed with **cellulose fibers**. It can be processed into a **thermoplastic granulate** and is especially suitable for injection molding. Because the material consists of wood components, it has similar mechanical and thermal properties to natural wood. This is helpful when attaching veneers because the expansion behaviors of the substrate and veneer material are highly similar.[54]

Ground **almond shells** left over from food processing can be used to create another ligno-cellulose material. It was originally developed as a wood substitute for coffin production. Over a million trees are felled in Europe each year purely to make coffins, most of which are then directly incinerated in crematoriums. The mass from the ground almonds is mixed with natural resins and mineral leftovers and then cast into forms. After hardening, the result is a durable and resilient material which can be sanded and drilled like wood and is entirely biodegradable.[53]

No additional binding agent is required in the fabrication of a material with cellulosic base substances that is compacted at high pressure like in paper production. Plant fibers or old newspapers can be utilized here—these are first processed into a formable mass and then compressed and dried to achieve high levels of rigidity. The fibrous mass can be formed and individually colored with vegetable dyes. The material is water resistant under normal conditions but disintegrates if submerged in water for several days or weeks.[50]

3.3 Biocomposites

In the "Light & Strong" chapter, we already looked at the technology of fiber-reinforced biocomposites, which are manufactured with embedded natural fibers or textiles via lamination. Here, the fiber alignment is customized to suit the load capacity.

Beyond this, there are natural composite materials characterized by a homogenous material structure that can be processed into semifinished products with standard compression molding equipment or extrusion machinery. One of the most important new material groups in this field is **wood plastic composites** (WPC). So far these have been more successful in the United States than in Europe. They are thermoplastically processed composite materials that are manufactured from wood or plant constituents (e.g. from hemp, hops, or flax) and plastics (mostly polypropylene PP or polyethylene PE). The wood content is between 50% and 90%. The materials are processed by **thermoplastic forming methods** such as extrusion, injection molding, or pressing.[55, 56] The material is then ideal for applications where good moisture resistance, high strength, and good formability are required at low cost.

As splinter-proof substitutes for local and tropical woods, WPC products are particularly suitable for resilient extruded products such as deck flooring—several versions are already available.[57]

55 — Natural fiber-plastic composite material in granule form for thermoplastic processing.

But the design aspect of this ecologically interesting material has yet to attract attention. Colors and textures mostly appear matte. The product marketing has focused more on the technical dimension—the material surface is frequently concealed beneath coatings.

The design studio Mehrwerk Designlabor in Halle has embraced this neglected design potential to create an intelligent shelf system. In collaboration with the Fraunhofer Institute for Mechanics of Materials (IWM) in Halle, they developed and evolved a prototype up to production standard. The system is made not of solid panels but of extruded hollow profiles. This saves weight, increases stiffness, and allows for wiring to be run inside the profiles. Furthermore, the hollow chambers serve to house the patented "insert and expand" connector with which the mitered side panels can be variably joined together to produce different configurations. The special fitting is barely visible on the outside. The material is 80% **wood fiber** and the rest is **polypropylene.** The design takes a confident approach to the material's inherent surface qual-

56 — Natural fiber-plastic can be formed into extruded profiles and can also replace materials with energy-intensive production, such as aluminum, in numerous applications.

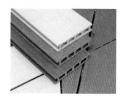

57 — Weather-resistant deck flooring made from wood plastic composites (WPC).

58 — Extruded hollow profiles made from wood plastic composites.

ities. The feel of the surface is reminiscent of natural wood and is protected by applying a thin transparent **PMMA** film that ensures a scratchproof finish.[60]

The visual and tactile qualities of a raw surface made of broken-down plant fibers is highlighted in the Pouf de Paille furniture piece by Tété Knecht. **Straw chaff** is combined with **latex** to form an elastic composite material. The "pouf" plays with the emotional component of hay that evokes memories. The material is flexible, pleasant to touch, and comfortable to sit or lie down on. The surface is made elastic by the latex additive and stabilized by the flexible fibers which provide the structural resilience.[61]

Plant materials have outgrown their "eco" image. Interesting design alternatives to conventional materials can be expected in future, particularly from the field of composites. Much of their charm lies in their multifaceted design possibilities. Even in the home workshop, one can experiment with vegetable starch and plant fibers to create new mixtures.[62]

Furthermore, these are materials with a future because their natural component reopens a door to materials that can be experienced on a sensual level. Thus, surfaces that are industrially produced with technical processes can suddenly reacquire a natural feel. These surfaces are never too perfect—they allow signs of wear or aging to be perceived not as defects but in positive terms as patina, revealing the product's history. Beyond all the scientific parameters that measure recyclability and technical properties, this could be the key to a widespread acceptance and thus to a promising future for renewable materials.

59 — Moss is placed on <u>3D fabric mats</u> made of PLA as a temporary indoor installation. Cavities in the bioplastic material offer an ideal structure for the fine roots of the green carpet.
Tokyo Fiber '09 – Senseware. Design: Makoto Azuma, Tokyo.

60 — Shelving made from wood plastic composites (WPC). Thanks to
the 80% wood content, the surface has a high-quality look and feel. It
can be combined into a variety of forms with the patented connectors.
It takes just a few minutes to dismantle and is easy to transport
because of the light hollow profiles. The prototype of the Extruso
shelf received the WPC innovation award in 2008 for the best market
application.
Extruso. Design & development: Mehrwerk Designlabor (Stefan Oßwald,
Enrico Wilde) Halle, in collaboration with Sven Wüstenhagen, Fraunhofer Institute for Mechanics of Materials IWM, Halle.

62 — Biopolymer tests made from rice and potato starch mixed with diverse natural fibers.
Molded Nature, Boisbuchet, 2008. Research: Studio Beat Karrer, Zurich.

61 — Seating cushions made from an elastic straw-latex composite material.
Pouf de Paille, 2005. Design: Tété Knecht, Switzerland.

Re-grown – Biocomposites

Glossary

Plastic recycling

Primary energy consumption in the production of plastic is high. The production of recycled plastics requires up to 80% less energy than the production of new plastics. Life span depends on various external factors such as UV radiation, temperature, mechanical wear, and weathering. To date, it has not been possible to gain much experience of long-term aging behavior in practical applications because many of the products have only been on the market for 15–20 years. The ongoing development of components and additives also makes it difficult to make predictions.

Plastics are divided into thermoplastics and thermosets. The principle difference lies in their molecular structure, which results in their differing behavior when exposed to heat—and thus to their recyclability:

Thermoplastics
(e.g. polyethylene terephthalate PET or polypropylene PP) consist of non-cross-linked long-chain macromolecules and can be melted down for recycling. The prerequisite here is that the collected material is homogeneous. The recycling of non-sorted thermoplastics or polymer blends is very labor intensive.

Thermosets
(e.g. polyester resins or epoxy resins) consist of tightly-knit, irreversibly cross-linked molecules. Thermosets cannot be recycled because they do not melt down.

Two basic methods of recycling are available:

Mechanical recycling
This is done via shredding or granulation of plastic waste. Homogeneity is critical here. The materials can be processed into new finished or semifinished products using conventional machinery for plastic processing. The polymer structure remains intact.

Chemical recycling
Here, the polymer chain is split up and broken down into its basic chemical components. Waste plastic can furthermore be deployed as a substitute for heavy oil in steel production. Converted into synthetic gas, it removes the oxygen from the iron ore and the result is pig iron—the basis for steel.
—page 204

Regrowing insulation materials

The insulating effect of natural insulation materials is based on air pockets in the voids between the fibers. The thermal conductivity coefficient is generally around 0.40 W/mK and is thus similar to conventional insulation materials. Borates (boric salt) can be added to the natural fibers as flame retardants and to protect against rodent and mildew infestation.

Flax

Obtained from the stalk of the flax plant. The short fibers are processed into insulation materials, while the long fibers are used in the manufacturing of linen. *Product form: panels, felts, and loose-stuffing wool.*

Hemp

A robust, fast-growing plant. Hemp insulation materials are manufactured from hemp fibers and shives—a by-product of hemp cultivation. *Product form: panels, rolls, felts, loose-stuffing wool, and blown-in insulation.*

Wood

Wood-fiber insulation is made from wood leftovers. The fiber material is compressed and bonded while additives are mixed in. Wood-fiber panels come in soft and hard versions. Sawmill leftovers and woodchips can be used as blown-in insulation. Wood wool is bonded with a cement or magnesite suspension and processed into lightweight wood-wool insulation panels. *Product form: panels, mats, and blown-in insulation.*

Cork

Cork is obtained from the bark of the cork tree and shredded into granulate. Stripping the bark does not harm the cork tree. As long as the material is harvested in an appropriate manner, the bark grows back. However, it takes around 10 years before the bark can be harvested again. For cork insulation panels, ground cork, or recycled material from bottle corks or production waste are expanded under the impact of pressure and steam. *Product form: panels or rolls, fill material.*

Coconut fibers

Obtained from the bast fibers of the coconut and compacted into a fleece. The flexible fibers are extremely resistant to rotting and can be deployed as thermal or acoustic insulation and also as a shock-absorbing material. *Product form: mats, panels, felts.*

Cellulose

Derived from cellulose fibers that can be obtained from recycled newspaper or plants (e.g. grass). The loose flakes are blown into cavities or applied to horizontal surfaces as fill material. For cellulose fiber insulation panels, paper is mechanically defibrated and compacted into solid mats on exposure to steam and with the addition of binding agents or binding fibers. *Product form: blown-in insulation, panels.*

Seaweed

Dried leaves are purified, chopped, and processed into mats or blown-in material. Seaweed balls can be unraveled and inserted into cavities. Due to the natural salt content, the material can be processed without chemical additives. It is fire and mildew resistant and highly durable. *Product form: insulation panels, blown-in insulation, loose-stuffing wool.*

Fungus

Fungus mycelia grow in fixed molds and they bind insulating perlite granulate and cellulose in the form of paper material or plant leftovers. Almost no energy is required in the manufacturing process because the insulation material "grows" at room temperature in the dark. In order to stop the growth process, the mass simply needs to be heated once to 43°C. *Product form: panels.*

Sheep wool

Sheep wool can absorb up to 30% of its own weight in moisture without any negative impact on its thermal conductivity. Sheep wool has fire-retardant properties by nature. *Product form: mats, felts, stuffing wool.*
—**page 219**

F
230 — 240

Appendix

Index

1.0
— Sources of material images

Index

2.0
— Sources of project images

Index – Sources of project images

Index
3.0
— Key words

Index

Index

4.0
— Architects/designers

Christiane Sauer

Christiane Sauer is a practicing architect and founder of forMade—office for architecture and material in Berlin. In addition to planning and construction activities, she works as a materials consultant for designers and industry. The focus of her interests is on innovative material applications and new material developments. Previously she has worked as a design architect for renowned offices and projects in an international context, including OMA Rotterdam on the Prada Store, New York. From 2001 to 2008 she taught at the department of design and building construction at the Berlin University of the Arts and is currently lecturing and giving workshops at various international universities. She is also cofounder of the Internet platform Architonic and regularly publishes in architectural journals and books on current developments in the field of new materials.

Index – Architects/designers

Made Of...

New Materials Sourcebook for Architecture and Design

Edited by Christiane Sauer
Text by Christiane Sauer

Layout by Daniela Burger and Floyd E. Schulze for Gestalten
Cover by Floyd E. Schulze and Daniela Burger for Gestalten
Layout Assistance by Ingo Neumann
Edited by Lukas Feireiss for Gestalten
Typefaces: Lyon by Kai Bernau, Foundry: www.commercialtype.com;
Planeta by Dani Klauser, Foundry: www.gestalten.com/fonts

Project Management by Julian Sorge for Gestalten
Production Management by Janine Milstrey for Gestalten
Proofreading by English Express
Translation by May Sander (Introduction), Wilf Moss (Chapters 1–5)
Technical Copy Editing by Daniel Wentz
Printed in Hong Kong through Asia Pacific Offset

Published by Gestalten, Berlin 2010
ISBN 978-3-89955-289-8
© Die Gestalten Verlag GmbH & Co. KG, Berlin 2010

This book has been printed on PEFC certified paper which ensures responsiblepaper sources with sustainable forest management.

Gestalten is a climate-neutral company and so are our products. We collaborate with the non-profit carbon offset provider myclimate (www.myclimate.org) to neutralize the company's carbon footprint produced through our worldwide business activities by investing in projects that reduce CO_2 emissions (www.gestalten.com/myclimate).

Bibliographic information published by the Deutsche Nationalbibliothek. The Deutsche Nationalbibliothek lists this publication in the Deutsche Nationalbibliografie; detailed bibliographic data is available online at http://dnb.d-nb.de.

Christiane Sauer thanks the IKEA Foundation for generously supporting this publication.
Thanks also go to Lukas Feireiss for his conceptual support and consultation on the project.